This is a full balanced account of the arg[...] of marriage to same sex couples. I comm[...] this vitally important question. The read[...] on this issue confident that it is base[...] dependent on any view he or she has pre[...]

**The Rt Hon the Lord Mackay of Clashfern KT,
former Lord Chancellor of Great Britain**

The support of same-sex marriage by our political leaders has almost inhibited reasoned discourse around this complex and sensitive issue. So this well-researched and measured publication is a timely contribution which offers light rather than heat with well-documented information. I commend it especially to those with open minds who believe in democratic debate and want to hear both sides of the argument.

**The Baroness Cox, former Deputy Speaker of the House of Lords**

This is a well-researched, balanced, comprehensive and marvellous study. I found it most useful in collecting my arguments together and getting so much great information on the whole background in an infinitely fair and extraordinarily well-reasoned way. It puts paid to those arguments made by same-sex marriage advocates which we thought were so convincing. The six essential components of marriage listed and explained by the author are a powerful argument that makes it absolutely clear that civil partnerships can in no way be deemed to be marriage. This study needs to be read by a wide audience.

**The Baroness O'Cathain OBE**

This is in the great tradition of British pamphlets – clear in its exposition, convincing in its arguments, it should be required reading for every politician, especially those well-intentioned leaders whose insufficiently thought out proposals could have the unintended consequence of undermining the very bedrock of our still stable family-based society.

**The Lord Cormack DL**

Marriage for me is a sacrament and a union between a man and a woman. This is an important part of my religious belief as a practising Catholic. The attempt to redefine marriage would have serious consequences for family life and indeed society. R. S. Harris has written a well balanced and thoughtful defence of marriage and I recommend this work as part of the wider debate that is taking place.

**Jim Dobbin MP, Member for Heywood and Middleton**

For some this study will not make for comfortable reading, but it ought to be read and studied by all. R. S. Harris very carefully appraises and challenges the arguments of those who seek to change the traditional understanding of marriage and its nature. I would encourage the wide circulation of, and proper engagement with, his careful analysis of the wide range of issues involved in a matter which will have implications for our whole society and its future.

**The Rt Revd Dr Michael Langrish, Bishop of Exeter**

R. S. Harris has been nothing if not thorough in his description and analysis of the issue of same-sex marriage. He points to the uniqueness of marriage as a publicly undertaken relationship between a man and woman for life and to the exclusion of all others. He shows how other relationships, whatever their value, should not be confused with marriage nor can it be said that the benefits of marriage would accrue to these relationships if they were. He considers the question of identity and cautions against confusing inclinations and desires with fundamental questions about who we are and what we are here for. His work makes for compelling reading and his opponents have a lot of questions to answer.

**The Rt Revd Dr Michael Nazir-Ali, former Bishop of Rochester and former Member of the House of Lords; President of OXTRAD.**

Healthy Parliamentary Government requires that those proposing legislation know that they will face robustly argued opposition. It is therefore thoroughly unhealthy that in the matter of 'Equal Civil Marriage' there is so remarkable a degree of consensus between the political Parties, not only in support of the proposal, but in the apparent conviction that nothing can intelligently and decently be said against it. So I warmly welcome 'Is there a case for same-sex marriage?' as a comprehensive and extensively-referenced contribution to the debate; and I hope that responsible Parliamentarians will read it and weigh its arguments.

**The Rt Revd Michael Scott-Joynt, former Bishop of Winchester; former Member of the House of Lords**

An important contribution that highlights that this issue is far more complex than at first imagined, and cannot, solely, be decided on the idealism of a few. Whatever one's position, Harris aptly demonstrates that the sensitivity of this issue may have been wholly underestimated by some members of the political-class and that formal equality is by no means an easy concept to grasp.

**Dr. Abhijit Pandya, Daily Mail blogger; Executive Director of the Centre for Democratic Studies; former Teaching Fellow at the London School of Economics**

Those in the "uncertain middle" who do not wish to incur the intimidation of activists for "gay" marriage, find it more comfortable to declare an ambivalent or agnostic position on the matter. R. S. Harris's comprehensive and evidence-based study argues that "equal marriage" fails the eligibility test for marriage and so is not discriminatory. His discussion on the related issues of children, and the legal position facing the churches will be illuminating for those not afraid to examine the evidence with an open mind.

**Canon Dr Chris Sugden, Executive Secretary, Anglican Mainstream; Member of the General Synod of the Church of England**

An excellent, valuable and fearless examination of the issues raised. It should be compulsory reading for all involved!

**Revd Lynda Rose, Director, Voice for Justice UK**

Important decisions about socially significant matters deserve very careful attention, and should come only after full and well-informed public debate. Here is a significant contribution to the debate. This well researched survey sets out in a measured and balanced way a range of considerations that should cause hesitation in UK political circles about the headlong rush to introduce gay marriage. It is not too late to press the pause button!

**Prof John Nolland, Trinity College, Bristol**

There is a disturbing, and growing, tendency to accuse those who oppose same-sex marriage of bigotry and prejudice, thereby intimidating them into silence, and effectively shutting down debate. In this study, the author reopens the discussion by spelling out, in clear and considered terms, why homosexual relationships are intrinsically different from heterosexual ones, and that the concept of same-sex marriage is in essence a category error.

**Prudence Dailey, Lay Member of the General Synod of the Church of England**

I commend this study because of its thorough treatment of the issues involved in the current debate. It has been well researched and documented and, on the evidence presented, its conclusions merit measured consideration by all.

**Guy Hordern MBE JP**

R. S. Harris does an uncommon thing; he brings reason into the ever present debate about the meaning of marriage and family. He debunks the argument often made that anyone opposed to same-sex marriage is bigoted. He explains the distinctive nature of marriage, and in so doing, demonstrates there is no compelling reason to redefine the institution...If we are serious about the future of our society and especially the future of our children, we would do well to carefully consider this well-written and cogent essay.

**Prof Dale Kuehne, Richard L. Bready Chair of Ethics, Economics, and the Common Good, Saint Anselm College, New Hampshire; Founding Director, New Hampshire Institute of Politics**

The quality of this research underpins a clear and objective presentation of the case for true marriage. Here is a compelling argument that the campaign to redefine it is pregnant with serious consequences for future generations. Children have an absolute right to the optimum environment for their emotional and social well-being. This study reaffirms the conviction that human dignity is particularly respected in the Christian understanding of marriage and is 'never in conflict with reverence for the Divine.' (Joseph Ratzinger) We are indebted to R. S. Harris for his timely publication as a reminder of the prophetic warning that families 'will be the first victims of the evils that they have done no more than note with indifference.' (Pope John Paul II Familiaris Consortio n44)"

**Edmund P. Adamus, Director for Marriage and Family Life, Archdiocese of Westminster**

# IS THERE A CASE FOR SAME-SEX MARRIAGE?

*Questions of Eligibility and Consequences*

## R. S. Harris

**ANGLICAN MAINSTREAM**
*in association with*
**VOICE FOR JUSTICE UK**

First published in 2012 by Anglican Mainstream
21 High Street, Eynsham, OX29 4HE, United Kingdom.
www.anglican-mainstream.net
office@anglican-mainstream.net

In association with
Voice for Justice UK
PO Box 3837, Swindon SN3 9DS, United Kingdom
www.vfjuk.org
info@vfjuk.org

A CIP catalogue record for this book is
available from the British Library

ISBN: 978-0-9575066-0-2

Cover Design and Typeset by TLB Direct

Printed and bound in the UK by Silveredge Digital, Poole, Dorset.
www.silveredgeprint.co.uk

**To my father,
Gerald Harris
(1932-2012).
Much loved and
always remembered.**

**The Author**

R. S. Harris read philosophy at University College London. He is a member of the Marriage, Sex and Culture Group (MSC) of Anglican Mainstream and works on a range of initiatives in support of family life.

**Acknowledgments**

I wish to thank members of the MSC Group for their encouragement. I am especially grateful to Dr Alan Loveless; and also to Alan Craig who first suggested that I write about the issue of same-sex marriage. I am also appreciative of certain people in the MSC Group who highlighted some helpful points or sources that were used in the final draft: Canon Dr Chris Sugden, Patricia Morgan, Dr Lisa Nolland, David Skinner and Dermot O' Callaghan. I am also deeply indebted to the editor, the Revd Lynda Rose, for her generous time and insightful comments.

# CONTENTS

## Chapter 1

### *Introduction*

## Chapter 2

### *The 'Love and Commitment' Argument*

## Chapter 3

### *The Legal Evolution Argument*

# Chapter 4

## *The Slippery Slope Argument*

# Chapter 5

## *Questions of Freedom*

# Chapter 6

# 1

## INTRODUCTION

## 1.1    Background to the Debate

Since the Civil Partnership Act 2005, same-sex couples who choose to formalise their relationship have been able to enter legally recognised unions which provide exactly the same rights and protections as those enjoyed by married couples. In spite of this some, though not all, gay rights campaigners, have insisted that a civil partnership is treated as a second-tier or inferior legal relationship. They argue that unless such same-sex partnerships are designated as "marriage", these relationships are not being treated equally.

The previous Labour government distinguished clearly between "marriage" and the new "civil partnership", but never attributed an inferior legal status to such partnerships.

In 2004, Lord Filkin, the government spokesperson for the Department of Constitutional Affairs and the Parliamentary Undersecretary of State, during a parliamentary debate, stated that the government's position was that "marriage should be possible only between people of opposite gender in law."[1] In a further clarification he said:

> The concept of homosexual marriage is a contradiction in terms, which is why our position is utterly clear: we are against it, and do not intend to promote it or allow it to take place.[2]

Three months after this government position was conveyed, Lord Filkin, during a debate on the Civil Partnership Bill, elaborated on the government's position:

> We do not see it as analogous to marriage. We do not see it as a drift towards gay marriage. We see it as having value, merit, meaning and purpose in its own right."[3]

---

[1] Hansard, House of Lords debate, Gender Recognition, 11 February 2004, Vol., 656 cc1093-5.
[2] Ibid.

It is noteworthy that no one seems to have accused the Labour government of homophobia or bigotry, even though it believed that same-sex marriage must be opposed because it is a contradiction that the law cannot recognise.

However, in the context of how opposition to same-sex marriage is now treated, Lynne Featherstone, former Equalities Minister, likened opposition to same-sex marriage as belonging to the "dark ages".[4] When responding to criticisms made by Christian leaders who opposed same-sex marriage, she urged her opponents to not use "inflammatory" language that "fan[s] the flames of homophobia".[5] Boris Johnson, Mayor of London, who supports same-sex marriage, suggested that marriage, as currently defined, is something that "needs to move beyond the Stone Age."[6] Indeed, to oppose same-sex marriage is now increasingly and commonly being placed on a par with incitement or provocation, with people in general feeling persuaded or culturally obliged to endorse the wide sweep of demands made by gay activists, couched always in the language of 'rights'.

Instead of a culture of genuine tolerance that is able to accommodate differences of opinion, Featherstone's comments – reflecting a politically correct position – are dangerously intolerant of difference and civilised dissent. Furthermore, her position, increasingly a view adopted by those in public sector roles and mainstream media, presupposes that there is only *one view* of equality that may be accepted as valid. This dimension of 'authorised' belief sits uncomfortably in a Western democracy that prides itself on being a leader in free speech, while openly purporting to celebrate diversity.

The Deputy Prime Minister, Nick Clegg, in a draft speech, apparently labelled opponents of same-sex marriage as "bigots", although he sought to quickly disassociate himself from these accusatory comments.[7]

In October 2011, the Prime Minister David Cameron, in his speech to the Conservative Party Conference, stated:

> Conservatives believe in the ties that bind us; that society is stronger when we make vows to each other and support each other. So I don't

---

[3] Hansard, House of Lords debate, Civil Partnership Bill, 12 May 2004, Vol., 661 cc115-80GC.
[4] http://www.pinknews.co.uk/2012/03/11/uk-equality-minister-churchs-opposition-to-same-sex-marriage-is-dark-age-homophobia/ 11 March 2012.
[5] London Evening Standard, 15 March 2012.
[6] http://www.independent.co.uk/voices/comment/boris-johnson-im-in-favour-of-gay-marriage-and-i-cant-see-what-all-the-fuss-is-about-8205338.html (10 October 2012)
[7] Daily Telegraph, 13 September 2012.

support gay marriage in spite being a Conservative. I support gay marriage because I am a Conservative.[8]

This speech marked an historic juncture not just politically, but also socially, with huge legal, educational, religious and cultural implications, in terms of how we – and all future generations - choose to view and practice relationships, family and marriage. It continues to provoke deep concerns among those holding to the centuries-old definition of marriage, namely an exclusive, sexually monogamous, lifelong relationship between one man and one woman. Such a traditional view, we understand, is neither 'owned' by any one religion,[9] nor those occupying the Right, the Left, nor those on the spectrum in between. Indeed, the institution of marriage, as a social unit carrying public recognition which brings forth the children of the next generation, has always been essentially apolitical.[10]

The Prime Minister's speech served as a prelude to the Coalition government's plans to introduce same-sex marriage into English law by 2015. Nick Clegg announced that it was not a matter of if, but when and how, the radical new law is to be implemented.[11] The government consultation[12] promised to confine the new proposed legal changes only to civil marriage, so that religious institutions holding marriage licences would not be permitted to conduct same-sex weddings.

However, advocates for "traditional marriage", warn that the advent of civil same-sex marriage will be a stepping stone that, due to equality laws, will lead to first permitting, and eventually compelling, churches to conduct gay weddings against their beliefs. This position is supported by influential legal opinions. These warnings have attracted reactions that accuse traditionalists of

---

[8]http://www.conservatives.com/News/Speeches/2011/10/David_Cameron_Leadership_f or_a_better_Britain.aspx

[9] See: *77 Non-Religious Reasons to Support Man/Woman Marriage*, (2010), Dr Jennifer Roback Morse. San Marcos, California: The Ruth Institute. www.ruthinstitute.org. See also: *It's not just religious people who oppose calling same-sex unions 'marriage'*, Daily Telegraph, Letters Page, 27 February 2012.

[10] It should be noted that some marriages, especially in royal and aristocratic families, are famously known to have been motivated by political or economic reasons. We should note that such marriages were not nullified in view of arrangements involving the wealth and status of the parties to the marriage.

[11] He is reported as saying: "These are proposals about when and how to open up civil marriage to gay and lesbian couples." He added: "It's not a matter of 'if' any more." See: "Tory opponents cannot stop gay marriage law, says defiant Clegg", *London Evening Standard*, 20 June 2012, p. 4.

[12] *Equal Civil Marriage: A Consultation*, March 2012, Government Equalities Office. The consultation closed in June 2012.

exaggeration or "scaremongering".[13] Eric Pickles, Secretary of State for Communities and Local Government, recognises these "legitimate fears" and has assured churches that explicit legal "safeguards" must be provided against any prospective coercion.[14] Yet one openly-gay government minister has already questioned whether churches can be legally protected.[15]

Some, though not all,[16] gay apologists judge it is sufficient that where two members of the same sex feel love for one another, and want to commit to each other, this is compelling enough to qualify for a "marriage" and therefore should be legally recognised as such. The underlying presumption driving such ideas is that unless same-sex couples have "access" to the institution of marriage, they are suffering unfair discrimination.

According to Lord Brennan QC, former chairman of the Bar Council, the word "husband" appears 1003 times in statute. "Wife" appears 888 times. "Spouse" occurs 2,740 times.[17] The total number of times "marriage" is mentioned in UK legislation is 3,258.[18] Lord Brennan argues that plans to change the legal definition of marriage could have "Orwellian" consequences. He points out that in the year after Spain introduced same-sex marriage in 2005, birth certificates referred to "Progenitor A" and "Progenitor B" in place of "mother" and "father". He asks whether similar rules will be implemented in England and Wales.

---

[13] See comments made by Margot James, the first openly lesbian Conservative MP: "Church Confronts Cameron over gay marriage", The Times, 5 March 2012.

[14] *A Christian ethos strengthens our nation*, Eric Pickles, The Daily Telegraph, 13 September 2012.

[15] Crispin Blunt said that it may be "problematic legally" to protect religious organisations from offering same sex marriage, see Daily Mail, 13 June 2012; Daily Telegraph 13 June 2012.

[16] It is not unusual for gay activists to object to the concept of "gay marriage". This opposition rests on the belief that marriage as an institution is based on patriarchal oppression, is sexually restrictive and is therefore opposed to individual liberty, especially sexual freedom, and is essentially an expression of heterosexual, family-centred society. Ben Bradshaw, a gay MP and former Secretary of State for Culture, Media and Sport, summed up the position felt by many gays and lesbians: "This is not a priority for the gay community, which already won equal rights with civil partnerships. We've never needed the word "marriage". See: *Daily Mail*, 14 April 2012. See also: "I'm a gay man who opposes same-sex marriage. Does that make me a bigot?" (Andrew Piece, Daily Mail, 13 June 2012.). The gay MP, Conor Burns, who opposes same-sex marriage, said there was "no clamour for this at all within the gay community" ("Gay Ulster born MP Conor Burns not for same sex marriage", 18 October 2012). See:http://www.newsletter.co.uk/news/local/gay-ulster-born-mp-conor-burns-not-for-same-sex-marriage-1-4381544

[17] Daily Telegraph, 14 March 2012.

[18] Daily Mail, 14 March 2012.

Official forms are expected to have the words "husband" and "wife" removed.[19] In France, where President Hollande made a manifesto pledge to legalise same-sex marriage, it is reported that the words "mother" and "father" will be removed from official documents.[20]

Although the government plans only to introduce same-sex marriage in civil law, some ministers and other senior opposition figures have voiced support for the rights of religious establishments to hold same-sex marriage ceremonies if they choose.[21] Counter-balanced against this, some government ministers have made public their opposition to same-sex marriage.[22]

In response to the government's agenda, the Coalition for Marriage (C4M)[23] was formed. The C4M website states that it is an "umbrella group of individuals and organisations in the UK that support traditional marriage and oppose plans to redefine it". In a petition signed, at time of writing, by over 600,000 people, leading signatories include senior public figures from different political parties, peers, legal experts, church leaders and academics.

## 1.2    Objectives

In this study, we seek to articulate a clear argument-centred and evidence-based case why marriage should retain its centuries-old legal meaning, while showing why what is deemed as "equal marriage" fails to satisfy the eligibility test and is therefore neither discriminatory nor undermining of equality.

Sometimes, intuitive objections to controversies involving sensitive issues of gay rights may provoke objections taking the form of "that is wrong". In the context of a mature debate, an expression of mere moral sentiment plainly lacks the components of argument. Equally true, and perhaps less acknowledged, gay marriage advocates can also frame their case in terms of sentiments in which robust arguments are likewise absent.

---

[19] Daily Telegraph, 16 March 2012.

[20] Daily Telegraph, 25 September 2012.

[21] 1) For example, Nick Clegg and Nick Herbert ("Clegg: Gay couples should have the right to marry in church"), London Evening Standard, 5 May 2012; 2) Ed Balls ("I back gay marriage for my uncle, says Balls"), Daily Telegraph, 30 May 2012; Yvette Cooper ("Religious figures meet at conference to back plans to legalise civil gay marriage"), Independent, 4 July 2012.

[22] Government ministers who have voiced opposition include Philip Hammond, Gerald Howarth and Tim Loughton, (Daily Telegraph, 14 May 2012); also, Owen Patterson, (Daily Telegraph, 11 June 2012).

[23] http://c4m.org.uk/

## Chapter Two

Here we consider what, according to same-sex marriage advocates, are now taken to be the two key defining components of a potential marriage: love and commitment. We examine why these two components are insufficient conditions that define "marriage". We explore what are six defining and enduring factors that constitute the basic meaning of "marriage" as an institution.

While different societies and religious traditions hold varying customs in relation to the ways married couples live out their lives together, we show that certain essential and intrinsic characteristics have, for good reason, always stood as conditions of *eligibility*, without which the relationship could not be deemed as a proper 'marriage' in the first place.

The meaning of monogamy is given special focus, especially with respect to how gay couples understand this concept in their own lives. We examine studies that assess what typically is the less monogamous nature of homosexual relationships. This claim counters the popular media portrayal that gay relationships typically hold an equal potential for monogamy with that of heterosexual relationships.

We also survey some of the studies that affirm the well-known fact that children achieve better outcomes when raised within intact, biological, two-parent married families. Crucially, we also take a look at the claim that children from gay and lesbian families do just as well as those from heterosexual families.

We study the right of children to "know" their identity by appealing to the UN Convention on the Rights of the Child.

While marriage is formalised in numerous ways throughout the world, we take a brief look at some of the main positions characterising how marriage is understood by the Anglican and Catholic churches.

A crucial part of this debate is to tackle questions about equality as a notion. What is equality taken to mean, and are there specific unintended consequences that inevitably follow?

Briefly, we consider certain questions and problems connected to people being labelled with respect to what is deemed their "sexual orientation". We also address undisputed medical evidence that throws a spotlight on the disturbing risks to which practitioners of same-sex activity are exposed.

## Chapter Three

We examine the claim that changing the definition of marriage to include same-sex couples, is simply an extension of evolving marriage reform that we have witnessed in this country over recent centuries. We argue that it is patently clear, in view of legal precedents concerning marriage law, that historical reforms never sought to redefine "marriage" in terms of its essential nature and meaning.

We look at the broad sweep of international developments and consider the impact of the UK government's desire to promote same-sex relationships abroad. We also ask how traditional marriage advocates might view same-sex marriage, in those jurisdictions where it is legal.

## Chapter Four

In the light of influential legal opinions, we question the government's promise to safeguard religious establishments from being forced to perform same-sex weddings, and show that churches are not immune from likely legal challenges from both European human rights law and UK equality laws.

We argue that gay marriage makes it more legally and culturally possible for society to be open to the concept of plural marriages, which includes a range of "poly" relationship arrangements. We show that the basic rationale used to justify same-sex relationships is broadly similar to the support that is likewise used to justify social and legal recognition of poly relationships and plural marriage.

## Chapter Five

We examine a broad range of actual precedents in which people have been penalised, investigated, or censored for expressing or endorsing beliefs about sexual ethics and traditional marriage. We also pay attention to current legal opinion: how will freedom of speech be impacted if same-sex marriage is legalised? We also address the likely impact on matters regarding education and the rights of parents.

## 1.3    Executive Summary

- With civil partnerships already enshrined into law, same-sex couples receive no material legal gains, should same-sex marriage be legalised. **(Chapter: 1.1)**

### Is Marriage Just About 'Love and Commitment'?

- Since eligible persons to a marriage can only be one man and one woman, this test is not about promoting discrimination or inequality against same-sex couples but about eligibility. The institution of marriage invokes obligations on those who enter it, which are not of their own choosing such as the obligation invoked on a father to care for any offspring. **(Chapters: 2.2, 2.3, 2.4, 2.11)**

- The concept of "equal marriage" is fundamentally flawed: 1) it wrongly presupposes a particular and questionable notion of "equality"; 2) it ignores the essential and defining components of marriage; 3) it erroneously judges parenting roles as interchangeable; 3) it wrongly presumes that the pool of diverse benefits known to married couples is *automatically transferable* to same-sex couples who "enter" the same institution. The distinctly different template of same-sex pairings means that we are not comparing like with like. **(Chapters: 2.2, 2.6, 2.8, 2.11)**

### Are There Essential Components Defining Marriage?

- Throughout recorded history and across the broad spectrum of different societies, marriage has been broadly characterised by six necessary, sufficient and enduring conditions. These are: one man and one woman; procreative potential; sexual exclusivity; permanence; mutual commitment and public recognition. **(Chapter: 2.4)**

- The government proposal legally to redefine "consummation" to accommodate same-sex marriage is not something that can be applied intelligibly to same-sex couples and is, therefore, a category mistake or mismatch. **(Chapter: 2.4.ii)**

- The government proposal to introduce "adultery" into same-sex marriage law is incompatible with what is being billed by the government as civil, rather than religious, marriage. **(Chapter: 2.4.iii)**

- There is no evidence that same-sex couples will benefit from the 'commitment device' invoked by marriage. Sexual monogamy, as it is understood by heterosexuals, generally holds a different meaning in the homosexual community, where those with long-term partners are often practising, or tolerant of, 'open' relationships. The less monogamous nature of gay relationships is demonstrated by a range of studies. **(Chapters: 2.5, 2.6)**

## What do the Studies Say About the Needs of Children, the Wider Benefits of Marriage, and Same-Sex Couples and Children?

- A wealth of studies show that children raised in married, biological, opposite-sex, intact families have overall better outcomes compared to cohabiting and single parent families. As for children raised by same-sex couples and how children are impacted, there is no comparable and credible social science data that can be examined against studies of married, biological, opposite-sex, intact families. The existing data on same-sex parenting draws on inadequate samples and flawed methodology and, therefore, cannot legitimately be used as a basis for comparison with children raised by married, opposite-sex couples. **(Chapters: 2.7, 2.8)**

- Same-sex marriage advocates commonly ask their opponents how someone of the same-sex, who is given the legal right to marry, can affect others. Same-sex marriage introduces a disturbing new norm into society, namely that children do not need both a mother and father for their optimal development. **(Chapters: 2.2, 2.7)**

- The UN Convention on the Rights of the Child affirms the child's "right to know and be cared for by his or her parents." Under IVF arrangements made by same-sex couples, children are deliberately denied knowledge of, and contact with, one biological parent. This is a grave injustice, for it excludes a child from one of his or her natural parents, and wrongly privileges adult needs above those of children. The roles of both a mother and father in the rearing of children are significant. **(Chapters: 2.7, 2.9)**

## Questions of Equality and Related Questions of Labelling, Orientation and Welfare

- Marriage is a basic and foundational universal institution, common to all societies going back thousands of years. Marriage also holds a distinct and unique place in Christian belief. Contrary to a Court of Appeal ruling, which held that the "orthodox Christian view" of marriage (as a union of one man and one woman for life), was not a core part of Christianity, it is foundational to Christian belief, defining the relationship of men and women with each other, and God. This judgment holds legal implications for the manifestation of religious conscience. **(Chapters: 2.10, 4.1, 5.1)**

- Law commonly allows for discrimination between different groups. Family members and unmarried heterosexual couples are prohibited from entering civil partnerships, and are thus discriminated against. If the "equality" promoted by government and activists is about equal treatment and ending the perpetration of prejudice, with the sole criterion for marriage being 'love and commitment', irrespective of gender eligibility, then inadvertent and embarrassing consequences ensue. A circumscribed acceptance of incestuous relationships is one inescapable outcome, especially between, though not strictly confined to, members of the same-sex. **(Chapter: 2.11)**

- Human sexuality is not easily classifiable according to 'orientation'. There is no automatic correlation between those who perform same-sex sexual acts and the labels 'homosexual' or 'gay'. The values and beliefs about human identity in people who reject the 'gay' label are written off as 'homophobia' by those who otherwise claim to embrace "diversity". Individuals, not society, hold the right to define their human identity.  If sexual 'orientation' is neither innate nor immutable, as is skin-colour, then the merits of 'class' qualification, for purposes of equality, fails outright. This conclusion holds implications for the equality doctrine as currently understood. **(Chapters: 2.12, 4.2.5)**

- Contrary to an apparent belief that homosexual practice is healthy, data from the UK (Terence Higgins Trust) and USA (CDC) reveal disturbingly and disproportionately high HIV infection rates among gays, bisexuals and men who have sex with men (MSM), despite such groupings constituting only between 1 to 2 percent of the population. In 2010, gay and bisexual men in the UK made up 69% of HIV infections acquired sexually, while in 46 states of the US, of the estimated HIV diagnoses among all males of 13 years and above, MSM accounted for 78%. Medically, it is known that, unlike the vaginal lining, the rectal lining is unable to withstand the pressure of penetrative activity, and it is far easier for viruses to enter the blood, anally. **(Chapter: 2.12)**

- Fear of causing offence makes society tread silently around the serious health risks attached to homosexual activity. Campaigns that discourage smoking are not interpreted as an assault on smokers as persons. Similarly, education about hazardous sexual practices should not likewise be judged as 'homophobic' but as a public health and welfare issue. Society should treat all people with equal and unconditional respect, irrespective of inclinations. But it is a wholly different matter to appeal to an "equality", which relies on a questionable concept of "gay" identity that is neither innate nor immutable. **(Chapter: 2.12)**

## The Evolution of Law and Related Issues

- Historically, marriage law has undergone reform. However, contrary to arguments that legalising same-sex marriage is only another evolutionary legal step in marriage reform, past reforms were essentially administrative in nature, and not about changing the intrinsic definition of marriage. **(Chapter: 3.1)**

- The British government's intention to promote same-sex unions abroad disrespects the beliefs, norms, and cultural and religious traditions of other countries. It is not the role of government to decide that it holds the moral and legal right to devise a new meaning for the institution of marriage. **(Chapter: 3.2)**

- While same-sex marriage can exist in law, in view of the fact it fails the tests of eligibility, its status would remain that of 'legal fiction'. **(Chapter: 3.3)**

- In light of influential legal opinions, government assurances that religious establishments will be safeguarded from being coerced to perform same-sex weddings remain unconvincing. Claims by government and 'equality' activists to support such exemptions, while denying similar provision to Catholic adoption agencies as 'undermining equality', serve to demonstrate a disturbing level of hypocrisy. **(Chapter: 4.1)**

## Poly Relationships and Plural Marriages

- Increasingly, advocates and practitioners of poly relationships believe they are also denied their rights to the same legal protections and benefits accorded to married couples. The rationale used to justify social and legal recognition of poly relationships (polygamy and polyamory) is essentially the same as those arguments made in support of same-sex marriage. **(Chapter: 4.2)**

- Gay activists and "equality" champions who advocate inclusion and diversity, act disingenuously when they distance themselves from the demand for rights made by poly practitioners, similarly claiming discrimination. This may be considered as indirectly promoting "polyphobia". **(Chapter: 4.2.5)**

- Countering the presumption that women are exploited in poly relationships, non-religious advocates of such relationships deny parallels between their egalitarian "post-modern" arrangements, and the historical oppression of women, believing it is not for others to "judge" their personal choices. **(Chapter: 4.2.5)**

- The apparent philosophy driving contemporary attitudes about sex is that individuals act from their personal, autonomous choices. Advocates of same-sex marriage cannot hold their position with any integrity, if they "judge" that those in poly relationships are "wrong" in wanting to share in the benefits provided by legally recognised unions. **(Chapter: 4.2.6)**

- Arguments from the legal world in support of polyamory being classed as a sexual orientation are being made by appeal to social justice, in some parallels to the historical development of gay rights. **(Chapter: 4.2.7)**

- The voices of poly advocates and practitioners are now being heard more regularly in mainstream academia, the media and the legal world. **(Chapters: 4.2.7, 4.2.8, 4.2.9)**

- Precedents for plural unions have emerged in the Netherlands and Brazil. **(Chapter: 4.2.9)**

## Questions of Freedom

- What were once conventional values regarding traditional family life, sexual ethics and marriage are now treated with a similar uncompromising intolerance once meted out to homosexuals and their beliefs. Dissent from the new orthodoxy about sexuality and marriage is now progressively treated with the same repugnance and intolerance as the US Senate McCarthy Committee once treated those suspected of supporting communism. Increasingly, the State effectively defines 'authorised belief'. **(Chapter: 5.1)**

- A growing body of disturbing precedents show that traditional freedoms connected to beliefs about sexual ethics and marriage are being challenged, sometimes involving the loss of employment, censorship or even police investigation. Should same-sex marriage be introduced, legal opinion suggests deleterious impact on education will be inescapable, with teachers and parents being legally compelled to comply with the new orthodoxy. **(Chapter: 5.1)**

- An emerging political correctness dangerously conflates questions about "gays and gay relationships", thus generating unwarranted accusations of bigotry. Self-identified "gays" are as much a part of the human family as any and every other individual. However, we sharply distinguish this from the question of what society chooses to hold as normative and leading to (or promoting) healthy relationships. In the gay rights context, as in any other matter of divergent opinions openly aired, disagreement is *not* hatred. **(Chapter: 5.2)**

# 2

# THE 'LOVE AND COMMITMENT' ARGUMENT

## 2.1    Introduction

The marriage issue can, and often does, provoke a range of strong reactions in people, which often seems based on personal feelings. It seems evident that at least some, if not much, of this, is determined by people's childhood experiences of family life. For example, some, who witnessed frequent parental infidelity, violence, or the pain of neglect, may be inclined to instinctively view marriage negatively. Marriage can be perceived as no more than a 'piece of paper'. Likewise, those who recall happy family experiences may be positively influenced. For the current purposes, we will concern ourselves with neither the quality of the relationship, nor with putting forward some kind of romanticised idyll.

In this study, we take "traditional marriage" not to refer to something that is merely historical, in the sense that it is old-fashioned, but as contemporary and useful to the lives of the modern generation. Many, if not most, young people in the world today aspire to having a lifetime partner and to building their own family. Couples setting out on married life together typically seek the stability and fidelity that is an expectation of married life.

The practice of faithfulness and monogamy is the platform on which the possibility of enduring trust between the spouses is developed. However, alongside this reality are questions about those attracted to their own sex, so in this current debate, we focus specifically on the question of same-sex marriage, examining related issues of equality, and the welfare of those contemplating or already involved in a same-sex relationship.

Some critics argue that traditional marriage advocates seek an ideal that is unrealistic, which suggests a lack of appreciation of the problems that arise for some married couples. Instead, our main focus and aim is to convey what the institution of marriage actually is, which opens up the question: what are the conditions of eligibility?

In the ministerial foreword to the government consultation on same-sex marriage, it states:

We recognise that the personal commitment made by same-sex couples when they enter into a civil partnership is no different to the commitment made by opposite-sex couples when they enter into a marriage. We do not think that the ban on same-sex couples getting married should continue. Put simply, it's not right that a couple who love each other and want to formalise a commitment to each other should be denied the right to marry.[24]

The two key components highlighted in the above statement are 'love' and 'commitment'. We will examine why these two elements, though now taken by some as satisfying the core essentials of a marriage, are clearly insufficient conditions to fulfil any intelligible test of a real and valid marriage. We also consider the place of sexual monogamy. In gay relationships, we ask what are the "rules", as far as sexual boundaries are concerned? And how do such rules fundamentally differ from heterosexual relationships, especially as relating to marriage?

## 2.2    Some Issues Underlying the Debate

There are sharply marked differences in belief between those advocating traditional marriage, and advocates of same-sex marriage. Both sides believe their position is non-negotiable. Maggie Gallagher, President of the *Institute for Marriage and Public Policy* sums up the essence of what is at issue on both sides and the implications flowing from the respective positions:

> Two ideas are in conflict here: one is that children deserve mothers and fathers and that adults have an obligation to at least try to conduct their sexual lives to give children this important protection. That is the marriage idea. The other is that adult interests in sexual liberty are more important than "imposing" or preferring any one family form: all family forms must be treated identically by law if adults are to be free to make intimate choices. This is the core idea behind the drive for same-sex marriage. And it is the core idea that must be rejected if the marriage idea is to be sustained.[25]

More recently, the concept of what is deemed "equal marriage" has made its way into this debate. This concept is used by the government in its consultation on same-sex marriage which is entitled *Equal Civil Marriage: A Consultation.*

---

[24] *Equal Civil Marriage: A Consultation*, p. 1.
[25] Testimony before the US Senate Subcommittee on the Constitution, Civil Rights, and Property Rights Hearing (2003). See bibliography.

The concept also features in the case made by Skelton and Flint in their paper[26] published by the *Policy Exchange*, a leading UK think-tank.

Same-sex marriage advocates believe that if equality is to be applied to all without discrimination, access to this unique institution ought, as a matter of fairness, to be made available to those of the same sex. This belief about equality also incorporates the notion that same-sex couples can and should have access to adoption services. In fact, since the Sexual Orientation Regulations were brought into force, this service provision has been enshrined into law. So, what is at issue here?

In line with many studies demonstrating the wide range of benefits enjoyed by married couples and their children, same-sex marriage advocates argue that if marriage were "opened up" to same-sex couples, they too, would reap *exactly* the same benefits.

We argue that the concept of "equal marriage" is fundamentally flawed. The concept wrongly presupposes a particular notion of "equality" as the foundational basis supporting the proposal of same-sex marriage. This is further examined in 2.11. Additionally, it ignores the essential components which define marriage, studied below in 2.4.

It is also flawed because it wrongly presumes that the pool of diverse benefits known to married couples are *automatically transferable* to same-sex couples who "enter" the same institution. This cannot be claimed with any plausibility, however, because the binary models under comparison differ categorically by way of gender. To put it another way, we are not comparing like with like. If gender holds no unique value marking itself out as distinct, then this might indeed provide one plank on which the "equal marriage" concept could begin to stand. Denying gender difference also implies that mother and father roles are obviously interchangeable – but both propositions are wrong. Men and women are not the same, but jointly make unique contributions that 'complete' their relationship, and it is for this reason that we speak of the complementary differences between a man and woman who are married.

If men and women are different, then that complementary nature is at once evident, so that the wider marital and parenting implications become obvious. Our culture once recognised this as a given, but we need not "go back" to a time when, for example, women were denied the vote and other basic human rights, to plainly recognise that male and female are not identical. At its most basic, men and women, by virtue of their biology, anatomy and reproductive roles, are different.

---

[26] Skelton, David and Flint, Robert. (2012).

Numerous social science studies indicate a strong relationship[27] between (one man, one woman) married couples and better health outcomes, as well as a fund of benefits to children, compared to those raised by cohabitees. However, the error is that we cannot simply *superimpose* empirical data drawn from the male-female marriage model onto that of a same-sex model. In the "equal marriage" concept, these considerations are not accorded their due weight and may be ignored altogether.

For social science purposes, the problem is that of moving from what *is* to what *will be*. The conclusion that may be drawn from social science data, (where sampling of married, heterosexual couples is used), cannot be presumed to legitimately apply to couples who would make up a different sample (same-sex couples). Accounting for the specific content of the sample populations being employed in this debate is more than important: it is good science that has regard for questions of research design and methodology. Ideological beliefs about how marriage can be newly devised, so that it presumes to replicate those benefits enjoyed by married men and women has no place in social science.

There are questions about same-sex marriage and it being "created" by legislative bodies. We believe state authorities are primarily responsible for, among other things, maintaining law and order. Government cannot legitimately use its law-making powers to change something as fundamental as the meaning of marriage. To do so, it would be usurping its functions and acting outside of its rightful jurisdiction.

Same-sex marriage advocates argue that the state should not place limits on who can have access to the institution of marriage. We argue that the state has no business in redefining the institution. Its role is solely one of recognizing those people who choose to live married lives.

## 2.3    What is Marriage?

With all this spelt out, what can actually be said of marriage itself?

Maggie Gallagher, when giving testimony before a US Senate Subcommittee, stated:

---

[27] There is an important debate to be had about whether a relationship between two entities is that of a cause (A actually causes B), or whether the relationship is merely correlative (A happens to be observed in relation to B). The social sciences are 'soft' compared with the 'hard' disciplines like physics. This opens up a range of important philosophical and social science questions.

> Marriage is in fact a cross-cultural institution; it is not a mere plaything of passing ideologies but in fact the word for the way that in virtually every known human culture, society conspires to create ties between mothers, fathers, and the children their sexual unions may produce.[28]

In *Sexual Desire*, Professor Roger Scruton, philosopher and writer explains:

> Marriage is a public endorsement of the passion which separates lovers from their surroundings. It is the public acceptance of their exclusive privacy. In entering a marriage they do not merely exchange promises: they pass together into a condition that is not of their own devising, and which contains the deposits of countless previous experiences of intimacy. Marriage, like every worthwhile institution, is also a tradition...which has been passed from generation to generation...[29]

By entering into the institution of marriage, a man and woman's relationship is being sealed with automatic public recognition of a newly created, exclusive relationship with set boundaries. The "condition" that is "not of their own devising" may be understood in the sense that the marriage relationship invokes mutual obligations to which spouses give their free consent. The institution into which the couples enter builds upon what Scruton calls the "deposits" of numerous former generations.

What, though, is an "institution" in the general sense? In his classic text, *A Theory of Justice*, Harvard political philosopher John Rawls, wrote that an institution exists when:

> ...at a certain time and place when the actions specified by it are regularly carried out in accordance with a public understanding that the system of rules defining the institution is to be followed...The publicity of the rules of an institution insures that those engaged in it know what limitations on conduct to expect of one another and what kinds of actions are permissible. There is a common basis for determining mutual expectations.[30]

In Rawl's definition, the "actions" of an institution are practised with regularity in accordance with an understanding of the rules by which the institution is to be followed. How might we apply this to the meaning of "marriage"?

---

[28] Gallagher (2003).

[29] Scruton (2006), p. 356.

[30] *A Theory of Justice*, Cambridge, Massachusetts: The BelKnap Press of Harvard University Press, (1971) p. 55.

According to the Church of England Submission to the Government Equalities Office, marriage, as a union between one man and one woman, is:

> enshrined in human institutions throughout history. Marriage benefits society in many ways, not only by promoting mutuality and fidelity, but also by acknowledging an underlying biological complementarity, which, for many, includes the possibility of procreation.[31]

On the role of fatherhood and its relationship to marriage, Bronislaw Malinowski, founder of modern social anthropology pointed out:

> the necessity for imposing the bond of marriage is…practically and theoretically due to the fact that a father has to be made to look after his children."[32]

Therefore, when children are conceived, one of the key obligations on fathers, invoked by marriage, is that they are morally expected to help care for their offspring. Marriage thus consolidates the bonds between fathers and their biological children.

## 2.4    Are there Essential Components Defining "marriage"?

There are many customs that have characterised the marriage relationship of a man and woman, not just in our Western society but throughout the world, in all periods of history. John Locke referred to marriage as mankind's "first society". Against this great deposit of cultural experience and legal tradition, are there specific, basic requirements that define marriage as an institution? We consider the following components which have endured as both sufficient and necessary conditions of a marriage:

|      |                        |
|------|------------------------|
| i.   | One Man and One Woman  |
| ii.  | Procreative Potential  |
| iii. | Sexual Exclusivity     |
| iv.  | Permanence             |
| v.   | Mutual Commitment      |
| vi.  | Public Recognition     |

### i.    One Man and One Woman

Throughout the world, marriage has always been broadly understood as the coming together of one man and one woman. It is important to

---

[31] *A Response to the Government Equalities Office Consultation* (2012), p. 1.
[32] Quoted in O' Sullivan (1992), p. 100.

note that in those cultures which recognised polygamous marriages, the template of the male-female binary was retained, even while an uneven numerical weight was accorded to the female parties. Polygamous marriages are still legal in some countries today. But in most societies, especially those shaped by Judeo-Christian principles, the marriage relationship is held to always be between one man and one woman.

In same-sex marriage, the implicit proposition is that gender is rendered meaningless for the purposes of a marriage. In contrast, the complementary nature of the male and female binary contributes its own unique value to a marital relationship. This complementary dynamic is also a source of richness and childhood nurturing experience for any children who are conceived.

However much a same-sex couple perceives their relationship as something that is enriching to them, this belief provides no more qualifying merits as a possible marriage, than any other non-sexual relationship or friendship that exists between two people. We know that the companionship element of any two same-sex persons can take multifarious forms (long-term friendships, work related relationships, sporting partners, those related through blood or marriage etc). But these many expressions of two people 'together' are a starkly different entity and proposition from that of a married couple of male and female.

## ii.    Procreative Potential

One of the great benefits flowing from a marriage, for both married couples and the wider world, is the prospect of children being born, so that a new family unit is created in society. Each family unit is a part of the global mass of families that not only makes up the human race, but guarantees the survival of the human family into the next generation.

Same-sex marriage advocates increasingly view their 'one man, one woman' opponents as backward-looking in their perspectives. To 'move with the times' is now commonly seen as a requisite by those who believe that progress is obstructed if we fail to embrace change. As for the current debate, it is only a man and woman who are able to generate children, thus ensuring that the planet's population is sustained. Whatever the perceived merits of same-sex relationships are in the eyes of its practitioners, one fact remains: same-sex couples, by virtue of what they lack, can never be procreative.

We know that some couples choose, for a variety of reasons, not to have children, even though they remain fertile, while some others, for medical or related infertility problems, are unable to have their own biological children. These scenarios are sometimes used as an argument to indicate that if some married couples cannot or do not procreate, same-sex marriage cannot thus be opposed on the ground that is fails to generate children. We believe this argument fails.

In a marriage between a man and woman, if, for reasons of infertility, no children are conceived, the *actual* procreative potential is either suspended or rendered inactive. However, in the case of same-sex couples, one cannot begin to speak about procreation being so much suspended or inactive. Rather, the possibility of procreation will never have existed at any point, nor can it in any natural capacity, without the artificial intervention of surrogacy arrangements, which – distinctively for same-sex couples - leave a trail of complications.

When same-sex couples choose to have recourse to reproductive technologies, for example, any children conceived are being deliberately *denied* knowledge of, and contact with, at least one biological parent.

Increasingly, in view of scientific breakthroughs, the spectrum of sensitive and ethical questions connected to IVF technologies and surrogate births is widening. This is another debate, the reaches of which exceed the remit of this study.

When civil partnerships were brought into law, the issue of consummation did not feature in the legislation. The government, through its current consultation, acknowledges that while non-consummation is defined with reference to marriage law, if same-sex marriage is legalised, "the courts may need to develop, over time, a definition as to what constitutes same-sex consummation..."[33] How could consummation, conceptually or in practice, apply in any intelligible sense?

The concept of consummation cannot be applied to a same-sex couple and is a category mistake or mismatch between subject (consummation) and object (persons). But even if we were to hypothetically devise a new concept, how would this apply, for example to women? In the case of men, it is well-known that acts of penetration are not performed by all parties, so what means could be used to apply such a concept? If not penetration, then what other

---

[33] *Equal Civil Marriage: A Consultation.* Para, 2. 16.

sexual activity would constitute consummation? This bizarre government suggestion invites a question to which there cannot be a meaningful answer.

### iii. Sexual Exclusivity (or monogamy)

Married people are expected to keep all sexual activity between themselves, meaning that no third party features in any sexual and intimate activity. This is a high standard. That this benchmark is breached by couples is sometimes used as an argument by advocates of promiscuity or cohabitation to show that this lofty expectation fails to reflect human reality, *as it is*. However, most couples who aspire to be married accept that monogamy is a required standard to be maintained. To breach this standard not only causes great suffering to spouses and children alike, but breaks the bonds of trust which serve as the basic foundation of married and family life.

Questions connected to the maintenance of sexual boundaries brings to our attention the potential tensions that can be very apparent between the *is* and *ought* of human nature. All advanced societies aspire to high standards of some kind. Morality, and the maintenance of sharply defined sexual boundaries in human relationships, is a fundamental centre-point that allows for the ordering of human relationships. The stability of this 'gravitational' centre-point bears directly upon the cohesiveness or fragmentation of families and communities. Casual sexual relationships may result in STIs, infertility, abortions and unwanted pregnancies, and there are often long-term emotional and financial burdens imposed on single-mothers whose children may never know their fathers.

People who object to marital monogamy would, in the words of Roger Scruton:

> have to believe that sexual pleasure can be treated as an adjunct to our personal emotions, something that can be tasted in any circumstances and regardless of moral or personal ties.[34]

According to sociologist, Patricia Morgan:

> Fidelity is at the opposite pole to transactions or relationships based on principles of contract of exchange – even if the

---

[34] *The Moral Birds and the Bees: Sex and marriage, properly understood* by Roger Scruton. September 15, 2003. See: www.nationalreview.com

current tendency is to see it in partnerships which can be renegotiated or reasonably wound up if the expected profits fail to materialise.[35]

How does the gay worldview fit into this notion of monogamy? Further below, we examine some important gay voices, together with studies that mark out different "rules" for same-sex fidelity. In the sub-section immediately below, we further examine the idea of sexual exclusivity together with the notion of permanence, as both are closely intertwined.

The government, in its consultation, states that the concept of adultery will apply to same-sex marriage, as it does to opposite-sex marriage. It will be for the courts to develop a definition as to what constitutes adultery.[36] While all societies have the concept of unfaithfulness, "adultery" is specifically a direct derivation from the Decalogue. We believe it is therefore incompatible that what is being billed by the government as civil, rather than religious marriage, should incorporate so intrinsically a religious concept as adultery.

## iv. Permanence

Marriage has long been understood as a lifelong and therefore permanent union. Choosing to live with one other person in sexual monogamy is not merely another 'lifestyle choice', since it is not something to be entered into lightly, compared with two people who may choose to cohabit.

Too often, we hear politicians and others present what they judge as the laudable notion of many 'family forms' that are becoming more apparent. We suggest that a relevant distinction here is between an "actual" or 'is' *and* an "ought" or 'preferred'. This difference may be judged as romanticising something that is ultimately not reflective of reality and must therefore be abandoned. If some people fail to remain in lifelong sexual monogamy, it is argued, why make sexual fidelity an absolute condition of marriage in the first place? This argument ignores two facts. First, irrespective of what one person might believe or feel about the merits or otherwise of lifelong monogamy, marriage is intended for life, and this has always been the widely accepted standard to which spouses agree. Second, if the marriage relationship is not deemed to be permanent from the start, this fails to create the

---

[35]Anderson, Digby. Ed. (1992), p. 99. See Chapter 7, Fidelity in the Family: Once Absolute, now Another 'Choice'.
[36] *Equal Civil Marriage: A Consultation.* Para, 2. 16.

economic and essential emotional security for both the spouses and any children conceived.

As for same-sex marriage, the 'till death us do part' component is being misapplied, and is therefore valueless. People can choose to stand in solidarity with one another for life, with varying levels of chosen commitment, but this unspoken or explicit agreement is, at most, a private settlement or arrangement between two persons. In contrast, when a man and woman choose to marry, they enter an institution that, as stated earlier, is "not of their own devising". Historically, it is a basic and foundational social institution that extends back to the furthest known reaches of recorded history.

In contemporary Western societies, people usually choose to marry on the basis of feelings of attraction, which makes it perhaps no surprise when the duration of marriage is challenged or comes under threat. Inevitably, the weakness in human nature means that some people fail to live up to some of their marriage vows: namely, remaining with their spouse for life. Further, the 'no-fault' divorce culture has facilitated – if not actively encouraged – some spouses to split, because on the one hand, less 'trouble-free' divorce is said to help end the suffering of couples whose lives are felt to have become unmanageable or intolerable; and, on the other, couples facing marital difficulties are arguably unnecessarily tempted by laxer divorce laws which hold out the promise of speedy escape.

v.   **Mutual Commitment**

Married couples are expected to show love, care and devotion to one another in both "sickness and in health". These commitments imply a sharing of any financial wealth or other assets that are held or created.

There is a differing emphasis in how the mutual obligations and rights of married couples are treated in various societies, where religious and cultural values differ in content and application.

Our own society places great importance in "being in love" as a pre-condition when selecting another person as a potential marriage partner. This 'condition' has not always characterised people's motives for marriage. In fact, even today in non-Western countries, what is commonly deemed as 'arranged marriages' may not involve "being in love" at all. In these societies, other family-centred or religious values are deemed to prevail over feelings of attraction or "being in love".

It seems difficult for Western attitudes to embrace these arrangements. We should clarify that arranged marriages do not automatically mean the two parties have not genuinely consented to the marriage. Those holding firmly to purist Western notions of autonomy and personal liberty may find repugnant the proposition of an 'arranged' marriage, even when genuine consent is not in doubt. Objections to all 'arranged' or facilitated matches, serves to highlight the difference between two opposing worldviews about the place of the self, within the setting of a wider community of people. In Western societies, while people are expected to be law-abiding, they are also encouraged to lead autonomous lives where life's priorities are shaped by individual preferences, choices, aims and tastes in lifestyle and belief. In principle and practice this may, and often is, at odds with the collective, family-centred community of values to which many non-Western people owe their primary allegiance.

According to Morgan:

> The Western conjugal unit may have enjoyed considerable freedom compared with those societies where it is subordinated to wider kin or absorbed into extended families. But with this went a heightened emphasis on marital loyalty and the indissolubility of the marriage bond by the law and churches. Marriage vows constituted a covenant (rather than a contract), or a promise at large, to all witnesses, including God, that the vows (for better or for worse) would be kept until death.[37]

Mutual commitments between spouses are not the only domain to which loyalty is directed. Mutual obligations potentially extend to the reach of other family members too. Primarily, obligations involving the nurture, welfare and education of children are the non-negotiable commitments expected of both mothers and fathers. The scope of commitment in specific areas of family life will vary from marriage to marriage. Beyond this, married persons' obligations to other kin, for the purposes of what constitutes a marriage, only hold relevance if a society's specific conventions and moral expectations recognise this as a moral duty. This wider ambit of moral obligations to kin does not add anything more to the essential mutuality of obligations existing between a man and his wife.

---

[37] Anderson, Digby. Ed. 1992, p. 103.

## vi.  Public Recognition

For legal purposes, the state of being married begins once a man and woman, before witnesses, make public vows involving their mutual obligations and rights, and officiated over by an appropriate civil registrar. Cultures throughout history have had differing means of conducting this public dimension. Ceremonies have differed in their content, duration and vow-making. Choice of venues, including who is permitted to officiate or the official means by which a public record is kept, has differed both in this country and throughout the world. The administrative means by which communities, both in the UK and worldwide, have recognised and given official sanction to marriages have differed considerably.[38]

Marriages in the modern world are typically recorded in national central registries. Historically, the public means by which marriages have been logged or recorded have varied. In this regard, we should have in view the fact that modern means of transport has facilitated a 'global village' culture of social mobility, whose scope is unprecedented in history.

Marriage is not a creation of the state. When two people choose to come together to be married, the state or community is merely *recognising* a state of affairs that is waiting to be lived out by the prospective spouses in their lives together. In cases where proper and informed consent has not been given by one of the parties, this is rightly seen as grounds for an invalid or illegal marriage. To this extent, the state may intervene in deciding that some 'marriages' do not deserve the state's recognition and are nullified.

By entering into the unique institution of marriage, the parties implicitly recognise that they form an integral part of that which embodies the wider community of families.

However, where two people choose to cohabit, which lacks public and legal recognition, this is not taken to be a marriage. Some senior legal figures attempt to argue that cohabiting relationships ought to be accorded some legal rights.[39] This apparent drive to bestow legal

---

[38] Lawrence Stone chronicles and examines three centuries of marriage law in *The Family, Sex and Marriage in England: 1500-1800*. This provides an authoritative treatment of, among other things, the administrative changes that the institution of marriage has undergone. See bibliography.

[39] See: "Give cohabiting couples who break up the right to share assets", (Daily Telegraph, 3 February 2011); "Unmarried couples granted new legal protection by courts", (Daily Telegraph, 14 October 2011); "Give cohabiting couples inheritance

recognition to such private arrangements devalues the institution of marriage in society, because it blurs the social and legal distinction between those who are married and those who are not.

This public dimension of a marriage relationship is key for at least two reasons. First, it is distinguished from mere private arrangements made by couples who suddenly decide to "move in together" or "move out". Private arrangements do not invoke the mutual, lifetime obligations that are true of matrimony. Second, the marriage relationship signifies to the community that each of the parties is committed to their spouse. This public fact serves to inform other people, who might otherwise wrongly harbour marriage or dating aspirations that cannot be fulfilled.

A secondary cultural component that often flows from the state of being married is to have that fact openly *communicated* to the wider community. For example, wedding rings stand as an outward and symbolic sign to others that a man and woman are married persons. In other cultures, there are other public signs demonstrated by the married persons to signify the fact that they are already married. For example, in Hindu culture women traditionally wear a red marking on their forehead (bindi) to indicate to others that they are married.

Outward signs may or may not, depending on the cultural norms in question, be regarded as a requirement by the conventions or rules of a society.

## 2.5    The Question of Monogamy

In the Policy Exchange case for same-sex marriage,[40] Skelton and Flint argue that if marriage between a man and woman acts as a "commitment device" – effectively altering behaviour and encouraging lifelong fidelity – then same-sex couples should have this institution opened to them too.[41] This argument is now increasingly used by same-sex marriage activists in an attempt to help validate the notion that same-sex couples can also enjoy the stability of lifelong fidelity, if only they can make public vows. Skelton and Flint appeal to a social science concept proposed by Michael Johnson. They apply Johnson's concept of

---

rights, say legal advisers", (Daily Telegraph, 14 December 2011). For a fuller discussion on this subject, see: *Marriage-Lite: The Rise of Cohabitation and its Consequences*, by Patricia Morgan, (2000), London: Institute for the Study of Civil Society.

[40] *What's in a Name?* (2012)

[41] Ibid., p. 13.

commitment in relationships, which he breaks into three separate parts. They argue:

> Without marriage, relationships are only held together by personal commitment [based on the personal satisfaction and pleasure gained from the relationship], whereas marriage helps to build commitment through structural [external factors like marriage vows], moral [factors based on a value system] and personal commitment.[42]

In answer to this argument, the following responses are offered.

First, Skelton and Flint appeal to a mechanistic formula that is overly simplistic and shallow, for the purposes of supporting the case for same-sex marriage. We cannot just speak of commitments based on structural, external factors, like vows; moral factors, like a shared values system; and personal commitments, based upon personal satisfaction and pleasure gained from the relationship. On this basis alone, we would be logically bound and compelled to "open up" the marriage institution to a limited number of incestuous relationships, even recognising polygamists and other poly relationship arrangements. This is considered further in chapter four.

Second, their argument bypasses and devalues the reality of gendered persons – male and female. In countries where same-sex marriage has been introduced, lawmakers typically refer to two "persons" qualifying for marriage licenses, as opposed to "one man and one woman". This apparent neutrality airbrushes the distinct value embodied in the gender of male and female persons.

Third, the personal, structural and moral commitments of a couple cannot be stated as the sole basis of building *marital commitment*, while the basic definitional terms of what constitutes a marriage are ignored altogether. When men and women choose to enter the institution of marriage, they cross a threshold into something that, as noted earlier, is not of their own devising. At this point, same-sex marriage advocates will have reason to ask: if we argue that marriage can only legitimately be between a man and woman, what do we make of the status of same-sex couples who, legally, are deemed to be married? This question is dealt with in chapter three.

What do gay writers say of monogamy?

The gay writer, Gabriel Rotello, wrote that, "Gay Liberation was founded...on a 'sexual brotherhood of promiscuity' and any abandonment of that promiscuity would amount to a 'communal betrayal of gargantuan

---

[42] Ibid., p. 13.

proportions."<sup></sup>"[43]   It is something of an "open secret" that the "rules" governing gay relationships differ significantly from that of heterosexual marriage between a man and woman, and cohabiting heterosexual relationships. This reality is in discord with what is extolled as the virtues of stable, same-sex relationships. For married couples, when one spouse has committed adultery, this is treated very seriously, causing deep pain, and often leaves a memory trail of mistrust. It may be cause for divorce if reconciliation is not achieved.

As noted above, there is a big expectation in marriage for sexual monogamy. But in gay relationships, this expectation is not typical. It should be noted that there are many same-sex couples who hope to be sexually monogamous, but this is rarely realised in the way that heterosexuals understand "sexual monogamy".

Many gay relationships are "open". This is when there is a mutual agreement made that permits one man to have sex with another man who is not his partner, on the understanding that he *informs* his partner of his actions. This infidelity can work in two directions.

In his influential book *Virtually Normal*, Andrew Sullivan, gay writer and commentator, states:

> at times, among gay male relationships, the openness of the contract makes it more likely to survive than many heterosexual bonds. Some of this is unavailable to the male-female union: there is more likely to be greater understanding of the need for extramarital outlets between two men than between a man and a woman; and again, the lack of children gives gay couples greater freedom. [44]

Sullivan believes that "something of the gay relationship's necessary honesty, its flexibility, and its equality could undoubtedly strengthen and inform many heterosexual bonds."[45] Sullivan argues that the lack of children in a gay relationship effectively frees the partners from the parenting commitments, bonds and obligations embodying a marital relationship. Sexual monogamy, for Sullivan, is too demanding for both straight and gay men and he argues that it is "mild hypocrisy" that serves a crucial role in maintaining the "social and marital glue". [46]

---

[43] Quoted in Diggs (2002). Rotello quotes from gay writer, Michael Lynch.
[44] Sullivan, (1995), p. 202.
[45] Ibid., pp. 202-203.
[46] See: "Two Generations", *The Daily Dish*, 31 May 2006.
http://andrewsullivan.thedailybeast.com/2006/05/two_generations.hml

Sullivan's argument that heterosexual relationships can learn from the "flexibility" of open gay relationships is not an isolated view. Anthony (now Lord) Giddens, pioneer of the 'Third Way' explains:

> marriage 'in the traditional sense' is disappearing, it is the gays who are the pioneers in this respect – the prime everyday experimenters.[47]

Giddens acknowledges that male homosexuals typically have a diversity of sexual partners, where contact is fleeting, and that male gays place in question what is traditionally the integration of marriage and monogamy.

If we were to suggest that married couples with children *should* enjoy extramarital outlets, so that sexual monogamy is no longer a standard, this would not just undermine, but destroy, the secure environment within which children are nurtured, develop their identity and learn about trust and relationship building.

As for the marriage commitment, if sexual fidelity as a requisite benchmark is removed, it no longer becomes intelligible to speak of "marriage" in any serious way. We may want to designate the relationship by another name, but it is not marriage within the ordinary, plain meaning.

If intentional sexual monogamy is a key component of a marriage, then we must *distinguish* between married couples who, through weakness, are unfaithful to their spouse, and couples who choose deliberately to enjoy extramarital outlets, believing it is their entitlement. This latter approach renders meaningless any marriage vows made.

As to the long-term gay perspective on marriage as an institution, Michelangelo Signorile, influential columnist and gay marriage advocate, imagines a future when the fight for same-sex marriage and its perceived benefits:

> once granted, redefine[s] the institution of marriage completely, to demand the right to marry not as a way of adhering to society's moral codes but rather to debunk a myth and radically alter an archaic institution that as it now stands keeps us down.[48]

## 2.6 Monogamy or Non-Monogamy: What do the Studies Say?

What do studies tell us about sexual monogamy in relation to gay relationships? We consider some of the studies ranging over several decades.

---

[47] Giddens (1992), p. 135.
[48] Quoted in Gallagher (2003). Originally published in *Out Magazine*, December 1994.

In a 1978 study[49] of self-identified gay men, the numbers of sexual partners were examined. It was revealed:

- 15% claimed between 100 and 249;
- 17% claimed between 250 and 499;
- 15% claimed between 500 and 999;
- 28% claimed more than 1000.

After the initial shocks of the AIDS epidemic that emerged in the early 1980s, the rates of promiscuity do not appear to have fundamentally shifted. In a study[50] conducted between 1982-1984, respondents reported having had an average of 4.7 new partners in the prior month (1982). Two years later, respondents reported an average of 2.5 partners in the prior month.

In *The Male Couple* (1984), McWhirter and Mattison[51] both medical doctors, conducted an in-depth study calculated to examine the quality and stability of gay couples. 156 male couples were selected, whose relationship lasted between one and thirty-seven years. Two thirds of the couples held an expectation of sexual fidelity at the start of their relationship. The authors, a homosexual couple, write:

> The expectation of outside sexual activity was the rule for male couples and the exception for heterosexuals. Heterosexual couples lived with some expectation that their relationships were to last "until death do us part," whereas gay couples wondered if their relationships could survive.[52]

McWhirter and Mattison acknowledged that when couples are sexually active outside a relationship, issues of trust and self-esteem arise. The authors explain:

> As a result of this study, we believe that the single most important factor that keeps couples together past the ten-year mark is the lack of possessiveness they feel. Many couples learn very early in their relationship that ownership of each other sexually can become the greatest internal threat to their staying together.[53]

---

[49] Percentage figures quoted in Diggs (2002), p. 1. This is from a study produced by Alan P. Bell and Martin S. Weinberg, "Homosexualities: A Study of Diversity Among Men and Women." New York: Simon and Schuster (1978).

[50] Quoted in Diggs (2002), p. 11. The study was conducted by Leon McKusicl et al., "Reported Changes in the Sexual Behavior of Men at Risk for AIDS, San Francisco, 1982-1984 – The AIDS Behavioral Research Project." *Public Health Reports*, 100 (6): 622-629.

[51] McWhirter and Mattison (1984).

[52] Ibid., p. 3.

[53] Ibid., p. 256.

On the wider question of monogamy, the authors further state:

> Sexual exclusivity among these couples is infrequent, yet their expectations of fidelity are high. Fidelity is not defined in terms of sexual behavior but rather by their emotional commitment to each other. Ninety-five per cent of the couples have an arrangement whereby the partners may have sexual activity with others at some time under certain conditions. Only seven couples [out of 156] have a totally exclusive sexual relationship, and these men all have been together for less than five years. Stated in another way, all couples with a relationship lasting more than five years have incorporated some provision for outside sexual activity in their relationships. Many of the couples have started their relationship with either explicit agreements or implicit assumptions about sexual exclusivity, which they have modified over time, finding emotional fidelity more enduring.[54]

These above points raise a number of crucial questions and issues.

McWhirter and Mattison believe that when heterosexual relationships endure, it is "possessiveness" that maintains the relationship. It is undoubtedly true that possessiveness features in some heterosexual relationships, as it can do in other forms of relationship, e.g. in work settings or family relationships between kin. However, we are at risk of missing the larger picture of what constitutes a lifelong and enduring man-woman marriage, by merely focusing on one characteristic that exerts undue pressure on some partners in married relationships.

In the context of marriage as a lifelong relationship, by directing the spotlight on one negative characteristic that can define some marriages, we lose sight of the other positive values that sustain couples in a life-long union. Marriage is not just about "special feelings" for another person, although sexual attraction and romantic attachments helpfully serve to "glue" two people together. It is also about making serious commitments to one's spouse, so that one also lives for the welfare of another person. While positive feelings for one's spouse can motivate or help incentivise commitment, feelings alone cannot be sufficient. Feelings for another person can, and often do, vary in quality and intensity over the course of time.

For a marriage to endure, a higher principle of devotion and commitment is called for, resting on vows that are neither taken glibly nor influenced solely by mere feelings of "liking" for another person. To the extent that feelings - not to mention sexual intensity - change during the course of a marriage, the

---

[54] Ibid., pp. 252-253.

endurance of the marriage must depend on the deeper intimacies that have developed. In this respect, trust, which is perhaps the main foundation stone of any successful marriage, cannot be expected to develop healthily or have much chance of being upheld, if infidelity is practiced as a matter of course.

In a 1985 study, *Sexual Exclusivity versus openness in gay male couples,*[55] most of the men who participated in a questionnaire study and who were deemed to be in "closed" relationships had at least one sexual liaison outside their relationship. They reported fewer sexual partners than those men in open relationships. The men in open relationships emphasised the benefits provided by sexual variety and personal independence.

Between 1994 to 1997, the US Centers for Disease Control and Prevention (CDC) reported that gays in San Francisco who admitted to multiple partners and unprotected anal sex grew from 23.6% to 33.3%.[56]

In 2005, research by Soloman et al,[57] found significant differences between the sexual attitudes, values and behaviour of gay men who were in civil unions and their heterosexual married male siblings.

Of gay men in civil unions, 58.3% had sex outside their relationship. Of their heterosexual married male siblings, 15.2% had sex outsider their marriage. Of those who had a "meaningful love affair" outside the relationship, 5.8% of gay men in civil unions reported the experience, while for their married siblings, it was 0%.

The findings state:

> This cohort of couples will serve as the pioneers for our understanding of issues that face same-sex couples in legalised relationships in the United States.[58]

The Couples Study[59] published in 2010 by Spears and Lowen marks an important contribution to our understanding of the practice of non-monogamy among same-sex couples. Taking four years to complete, Spears and Lowen set out to better understand the experience of non-monogamous couples. The couples were interviewed by the San Francisco State University. The chosen population only included non-monogamous couples. This deliberate selection obviously raises questions of methodology. However, its value can be seen in

---

[55] Blasband and Peplau (1985).
[56] Quoted in Diggs (2002), p. 1.
[57] Soloman (2005).
[58] Ibid., p. 574.
[59] Spears and Lowen (2010). See bibliography.

the information it provides of those for whom non-monogamy is a defining way of life.

Participants who were recruited had to be in a 'long-term committed relationship' defined arbitrarily by the researchers as 8 years or more, and to have practiced "'outside sex' or an agreement for such". Participants were recruited haphazardly through the gay community. The average age was 51, the youngest being 33, the oldest, 81. Participant couples had been in their relationships from between 8 to 42 years. 86 couples participated.

From the beginning of the relationship, thirty-six percent of the couples were "open"; twelve percent were "slightly open" and actually increased being open over the course of time. Forty-two percent of couples who were initially monogamous, opened their relationship "considerably over time". A small number of the couples (four percent) were initially monogamous but opened their relationship slightly. Six-percent of the couples actually moved closer to monogamy and away from practising open relationships.

Forty-two percent of couples had agreed to conduct their relationship as open within the first-three months. Twenty percent of couples conveyed that they were seeing someone, without prior agreement and then having to "come clean". "Often the catalyst was a partner getting 'caught', followed by heated arguments and a traumatic owning up. This was not an approach any of these couples recommended."[60]

In fourteen percent of cases, one of the partners "insisted, advocated, cajoled or nudged the other in the direction of non-monogamy".[61] A small number of six percent were unable to "fully resolve the issue of whether or not to open the relationship. This can result in on-going conflict..."[62] For an unspecified number of couples, the openness of the relationship "just seemed to show up quite organically as part of their evolution..."[63]

Spears and Lowen explain:

> When partners find enough common ground in their inclinations and perspectives toward non-monogamy, sanctioned outside sex is a sustainable and satisfying possibility.[64]

They further add:

---

[60] Ibid., p. 6.
[61] Ibid., p. 5.
[62] Ibid., p. 7.
[63] Ibid., p. 6.
[64] Ibid., p. 72.

If a couple is willing to be forthright and to problem-solve as needed, non-monogamy isn't by nature de-stabilizing. In fact, the results of this study would suggest the opposite – many study couples said non-monogamy enabled them to stay together.[65]

Of the fact that there were difficulties in the recruitment of couples for the study, and in view of these couples being together for an average of sixteen years, according to the authors, this figure suggests there to be:

> a positive correlation between longevity and non-monogamy. At a minimum, it destroys the myth that opening the relationship is the 'beginning of the end'.[66]

In addition, they explain that their study challenges what they believe is another myth, namely, that open relationships are "somehow less – less healthy, less loving, less responsible".[67] They judge the study's results as suggesting the opposite.

In their evaluation of the couples, Spears and Lowen believe that non-monogamous relationships provide a "valuable and satisfying outlet", permitting the men to, what they describe as, 'follow[ing] their nature', while coming to terms with varying needs, and also seeking "variety without jeopardizing their relationship".[68]

The authors of the study confess having felt reluctance in publicly addressing the issue of non-monogamy. Their worry was that bringing this issue to the public's attention would be perceived as, "jeopardizing the push for gay marriage".[69]

More frequently, politicians and champions of the new doctrine of equality refer to the stabilising effect of marriage, implying that if gays had access to this institution, their promiscuity would diminish. This belief erroneously presupposes two key assumptions. First, that the "rules" of gay culture are the same as that of heterosexual culture. On balance, the evidence demonstrates they are not. Second, the institution of marriage, being a formalised relationship between one man and one woman with specific boundaries, obligations and commitments, cannot be automatically *transferred* onto the template of same-sex pairings. It is not comparing like with like, even though the need for companionship is a basic human need.

---

[65] Ibid., p. 72.

[66] Ibid., p. 72.

[67] Ibid., p. 72.

[68] Ibid., p. 72.

[69] Ibid., p. 75.

In every human society, companionship commonly finds its outlet in friendships with a variety of people, irrespective of their perceived or self-designated sexual identity or "orientation". Our society now makes much of the perceived or designated sexual "orientation" of men and women.

## 2.7 The Needs of Children and the Wider Benefits of Marriage: What do the Studies Say?

Numerous studies have been conducted which show that children clearly benefit in a wide range of respects when their parents are married. Married couples also hold greater chances of staying together compared to cohabiting couples. We consider several overviews of the consensus that children profit best when raised by a married mother and father. In the subsection further below, we also consider the case that purports to show that children suffer no disadvantages when being raised by same-sex parents.

According to a 2009 report published by the *Centre for Social Justice*:

> married couples are far less likely to break up than couples who live together without getting married even after adjusting for the influence of such factors as income, age and education. Data shows that only 8 percent of married parents, compared to 43 percent of unmarried parents, had separated before their child's fifth birthday. The empirical evidence...shows that intact marriages tend to provide more beneficial outcomes for adults and children than cohabitation and single parenthood. Children tend to do better in the areas of physical and emotional health, educational achievement, financial security and their ability to form their own future stable families. Despite this clear and overwhelming evidence, there has been a lamentable lack of active government and parliamentary support for marriage...[70]

The above summary captures well the fact that married couples benefit children, while also showing that married couples – as opposed to those cohabiting – are more likely to stay together.

In a 2001 report, the US Center for Disease Control commented:

> Marriage is associated with a variety of positive outcomes, and dissolution of marriage is associated with negative outcomes for men, women, and their children.[71]

---

[70] *Breakthrough Britain*, (2009), p. 4.
[71] Quoted in Gallagher (2004).

The research literature was summarised in 2002 by twelve leading family scholars who stated:

> Marriage is an important social good associated with an impressively broad array of positive outcomes for children and adults alike. [72]

They concluded that:

> Marriage is more than a private emotional relationship. It is also a social good. Not every person can or should marry. And not every child raised outside of marriage is damaged as a result. But communities where good-enough marriages are common have better outcomes for children, women, and men than do communities suffering from high rates of divorce, unmarried childbearing, and high-conflict or violent marriages. [73]

In a research brief, the scholarly consensus was summed this way:

> research clearly demonstrates that family structure matters for children, and the family structure that helps children the most is a family headed by two-biological parents in a low-conflict marriage. Children in single-parent families, children born to unmarried mothers, and children in stepfamilies or cohabiting relationships face higher risks of poor outcomes than do children in intact families headed by two biological parents. Parental divorce is also linked to a range of poorer academic and behavioral outcomes among children. There is thus value for children in promoting strong, stable marriages between biological parents. [74]

In view of the social science evidence, the pro-traditional marriage advocate, Maggie Gallagher offers this conclusion:

> While scholars continue to disagree about the size of the marital advantage ... [and the means by which this is given] ... the weight of social science evidence strongly supports the idea that family structure matters and that the family structure that is most protective of child well-being is the intact, biological, married family. [75]

Same-sex marriage advocates now commonly ask of their opponents how someone of the same-sex, who is given the legal right to marry, can affect those who choose to marry someone of the opposite sex. When Maggie Gallagher

---

[72] Doherty et al (2002), p. 6.

[73] Ibid., (2002), p. 18.

[74] Moore et al (2002), p. 6.

[75] Gallagher (2004).

gave her testimony before a US Senate Subcommittee, she stated this often made complaint as follows:

> this translates into the question: how can Bob and James's marriage possibly affect Rob and Sue's marriage?[76]

While having regard to the available evidence and arising issues, Gallagher answered:

> Marriage is not just a legal construct; it is socially and culturally a child-rearing institution, the place where having children and creating families is actually encouraged, rather than merely tolerated. In endorsing same-sex marriage, law and government will thus be making a powerful statement: our government no longer believes children need mothers and fathers. Two fathers or two mothers are not only just as good as a mother and father, *they are just the same.*[77]

Gallagher further explains:

> this new idea of marriage, sanctioned by law and government, will certainly have a dramatic effect on the next generation's attitudes towards marriage, childbearing, and the importance of mothers and fathers. If two mothers are just the same as a mother and father, for example, why can't a single mother and her mother do just as well as a married mom and dad?[78]

In other words, legally sanctioning same-sex marriage means that children reared by two fathers or two mothers is treated as a new norm; furthermore, it wrongly renders the parenting roles of mother and father as interchangeable, and therefore without their unique respective value.

Having surveyed the consensus that children profit most when raised by their two-parent families, we now analyse the opposite view, that children raised by same-sex couples suffer no adverse effects and even profit as much as those with opposite sex, married parents.

## 2.8    Studies of Same-Sex Couples and Children

As to those who argue that children of same-sex couples perform no worse than their counterparts raised by biological, married couples, we are mindful of a

---

[76] Gallagher (2003)
[77] Ibid. Author's emphasis.
[78] Ibid.

wealth of problems that immediately arise. These include, but are not limited to the problems set out below.

When results of a specific study or collections of studies are used to *compare* the results of other studies, good social science demands that we are comparing like with like. It is not enough to show the possible similarity of conclusions or data between two apparently comparative studies. The population samples used in the comparative studies must be sufficiently close, if fair, meaningful and scholarly comparisons are to be drawn. Without identical or at least proximate sampling between comparative studies, there are obvious discrepancies in methodology, so that we cannot reasonably speak of comparisons between the studies.

Gay men and lesbians sometimes have recourse to IVF treatments. In jurisdictions where this medical intervention is paid for,[79] questions arise that bear upon the population sample of the same-sex parents. For example, if IVF treatments are costly, as they sometimes are, only lesbians of a certain socio-economic background will have any chance of accessing the services. Facts like these will immediately skew the population sampling, when we draw parallels with parents drawn from a different, wider socio-economic pool.

The studies that deal with the children of same-sex parents are numerically few and, quite apart from the methodology concerns, we do not have a sufficient body of data to draw the broad conclusions that same-sex marriage advocates make.

In 2005, the *American Psychological Association* (APA) released an official position on gay and lesbian parenting which claimed:

> Not a single study has found children of lesbian or gay parents to be disadvantaged in any significant respect relative to children of heterosexual parents.[80]

The APA stated its objective as one of influencing family law; the publication's focus is to "serve the needs of psychologists, lawyers, and parties in family law cases". Since this public stance from the APA, gay parenting advocates have appealed to this official position and made use of it in legal proceedings. Lawmakers and politicians have quoted it regularly to establish the case for gay and lesbian parenting.

---

[79] In England and Wales, lesbians are now able to receive IVF treatment, paid for by the NHS, irrespective of whether they are single or with a same-sex partner. The availability of this service was strengthened by a statutory provision that effectively ended the legal recognition that regard must be had for a child's need for a father.

[80] Patterson, C.J., 2005. *Lesbian and gay parents and their children: summary of research findings*. Lesbian and Gay Parenting, (American Psychological Association).

According to Loren Marks,[81] of Louisiana State University, 77% of the 59 same-sex parenting studies used by the APA were based on non-representative, small, volunteer or convenience samples. One had 11 subjects, the other only 15. The combined sample total from all 59 studies added up to only 7800 subjects.

On the problem of using random sampling, one psychologist who has served on the APA's Council of Representatives has observed:

> It is probably still true to say that no one "knows what a random sample of the homosexual population would be like; and even if one knew, it would be extremely difficult, if not impossible, to obtain one." So, how can assertions be made about homosexual parents in general until we are assured that we have a representative sample of these persons?[82]

When small samples are used, with imprecise methodology and variables that are uncontrolled or unaccounted for, these problems make it more likely that a Type II error is at play. This statistical concept involves a messy, random collection of 'bits' of data where it is possible to achieve a "no difference" outcome. By way of comparison, in many of the studies that address heterosexual families, findings come from samples of tens of thousands of participants that control for a diverse collection of factors.

In 33 of the 59 APA studies studied by Marks, a heterosexual comparison group was used (44.1% lacked controls). In those cases where heterosexual control groups were used, these were predominantly lone mothers, while there were a few cases of lone fathers. All of this is noteworthy, because children with single-parents are more likely to experience problems compared to those living in intact families with their two biological parents.

Of those other studies that made use of heterosexual control groups, references were made to "mothers" or "couples". We are not provided with information as to their actual status: were they married, single, divorced, remarried or cohabiting?

Marks asks how many of the studies cited by the APA specifically addressed the outcomes of children from "gay fathers"? Gay fathers were only referred to

---

[81] Marks (2012).
[82] Jones, S.L, "Sexual orientation and reason: On the implications of false beliefs about homosexuality," digitally published at www.christianethics.org; an abbreviated version of this essay was published as "Same-sex science," *First Things,* February, 2012, pp. 27-33.

in eight of the 59 APA studies. A heterosexual comparison group was absent in four of these.

Marks observes it "is noteworthy that all ...outcomes of societal-level concern are absent" from the APA studies list on matters of drug taking, labour force participation, criminality, education, childbearing and so on.[83] These effects are often not ideally observable until mid-late adolescence or early adulthood. It is significant to note that virtually none of the APA studies actually addressed longer-term outcomes.

We believe that in view of the plainly flawed methodology underlying these gay parenting studies, legislators and others in public life should be more careful in concluding anything major about the effectiveness of gay and lesbian parenting.

*Stonewall*, the UK's leading gay rights organisation, published findings that looked at the experiences of children and young people with lesbian and gay parents.[84]  In *Different Families*, 82 people between the ages of four and twenty-seven were interviewed from England, Wales and Scotland. *Stonewall* commissioned the *Centre for Family Research* at the University of Cambridge. Ben Summerskill, Chief Executive of *Stonewall*, claims that the research:

> provides [a] pioneering understanding of the current experience of the children of lesbian and gay parents. Many come from families which look remarkably like everyone else's.[85]

The interviews were conducted by two people. We are not provided with information about the reporting techniques used, nor are we told about any social science data about the socio-economic background of the parents. Neither do we know anything meaningful of the parents of these children.

One critical response to the above concerns is to simply recognise that the research was only ever intended to ask young people what experiences they had. The issue is that these reports can and are used as evidence to show that children are not adversely affected when they are raised by lesbian or gay parents. While the report does not claim to be academic or scientific in terms of social science, we should recognise it as no more than anecdotal reports. They tell us nothing of a social science value.

---

[83] Marks (2012), p. 744.
[84] Guasp (2010).
[85] Ibid., p. 2.

## 2.9     The UN Convention on the Rights of the Child

In the *UN Convention on the Rights of the Child* (1990), three Articles seem to hold special value in view of the current focus, namely, the rights of children, and how the state authorities are required to meet certain obligations designed to protect the welfare of children and their sense of identity, including parental identity.

The Convention enshrines specific rights of children into international law. It defines those universal principles and standards regarding the status of children throughout the world. The Articles we consider ought to be read in the context of certain principles stated in the Convention Preamble.

In the Preamble, the Convention contextualises the well-being of children as being allowed to develop within the family environment:

> Convinced that the family, as the fundamental group of society and the natural environment for the growth and well-being of all its members and particularly, should be afforded the necessary protection and assistance so that it can fully assume its responsibilities in the community,
>
> Recognising that the child, for the full and harmonious development of his or her personality, should grow up in a family environment...

The articles declare, among other points, that the "best interests" of a child are a primary consideration, and that a child holds the "right to know" and "be cared for" by his parents.

Article 3 (1) states:

> In all actions concerning children, whether undertaken by public or private social welfare institutions, courts of law, administrative authorities or legislative bodies, the best interests of the child shall be a primary consideration.

Article 7 (1) makes it an obligation that:

> The child shall be registered immediately after birth and shall have the right from birth to a name, the right to acquire a nationality and, as far as possible, the right to know and be cared for by his or her parents.

Article 8 (1) declares:

States parties undertake to respect the right of the child to preserve his or her identity, including nationality, name and family relations as recognised by law without unlawful interference.

Article 8 (2) requires that:

Where a child is illegally deprived of some or all of the elements of his or her identity, States parties shall provide appropriate assistance and protection, with a view to re-establishing speedily his or her identity.

In view of these Articles, what questions arise in the debate over same-sex marriage?

We address several points, against the backdrop of these Articles.

The child's "right to know and be cared for by his or her parents" (Article 7 (1)) cannot be read in isolation from the Preamble text which states decisively that the family is the natural environment for the child's growth and for his or her "full and harmonious development" of personality. A close link is being drawn between the importance of the family environment and a child's "well-being".

As to the parenting environment provided by a same-sex couple, is a child's right as declared in Article 7 (1) being met? The plain reading of "right to know and be cared for by *his* or *her* parents" can only refer, as we understand it, to a child's biological parents. Other possibilities, such as adoptive or foster parents who are clearly parents for many children, are not the meaning that is implied by "*his* or *her* parents".

Article 8 (2) places an obligation on States to ensure that where a child is "illegally deprived of some or all of the elements of his or her identity", speedy, remedial action is required so that a child's identity is re-established. In the case of children who are conceived through IVF, and then parented by a same-sex couple, so that the child is excluded from one of his or her natural parents, this may lead to permanent alienation between the child and one of his or her biological parents. It would depend on whether the sperm or egg donor remains anonymous. This deliberate separation of a child from one of his natural parents is favouring adult-centred needs over that of a child's rights. We believe this is a grave injustice.

Critics of our position may want to point to the fact that adoption as a practice (as opposed to IVF) has existed for thousands of years and no one has been bothered by this arrangement. Adoption can be traced back to ancient times, but there is a sharp difference between a child being adopted, and a child being conceived deliberately so that it will never know and/or be raised by one of the natural parents. In the case of ordinary adoption, children are given a remedial arrangement in a case that is already unfortunate. Children may have been "unplanned", or removed by local authorities because of parental incompetence. Or one or both parents may have died. In all these scenarios, adoption is remedial so that the child is given the chance of being parented. However, in cases where a child is created through IVF by same-sex couples, in the *deliberate* knowledge that one parent will be potentially cut out from the child's life, this we see as an injustice that discriminates against the child's right to both "know" and be "cared for by his or her parents".

How does this all fit into our own political landscape?

When children are conceived in a way that deliberately separates the child from one of his or her natural parents, it turns children into what was once described as "trophies". The former Home Secretary Jack Straw, stated:

> I am not in favour of gay couples seeking to adopt children because I question whether that is the right start in life. We should not see children as trophies.

> Children in my judgment, and I think it's the judgment of almost everyone including single parents, are best brought up where you have two natural parents in a stable relationship. There's no question about that. What we know from the evidence is that, generally speaking, that stability is more likely to occur where the parents are married than when they are not.[86]

More recently, Jack Straw, as with so many questionable political conversions on matters of gay rights, has declared his public support for same-sex marriage.[87] This change almost certainly suggests he has probably rejected his earlier objection to gay parents adopting children.

David Cameron, months before he entered Downing Street, declared that:

> the ideal adoption is finding a mum and dad, but there will be occasions when gay couples make very good adoptive parents. So I support gay adoption.[88]

---

[86] *Today* Programme, 4 November 1998. Quoted in *Children as Trophies: Examining the evidence on same-sex parenting*, p. 7. Patricia Morgan (2002). Newcastle upon Tyne: The Christian Institute.
[87] London Evening Standard, 25 May 2012.
[88] http://www.independent.co.uk/news/uk/politics/lets-talk-about-sex-johann-hari-grills-david-cameron-over-gay-rights-1888688.html (4 February 2010)

It is noteworthy that Cameron judges that the ideal placement of children is when the parents are male and female. It is unclear whether his position has since changed.

The UN Convention should, of course, not be studied in isolation from those studies that examine the role of both parents in the lives of children. In a recent study examining the cases of more than 10,000 sons and daughters, it was found that the presence of a father is as important as that of a mother. Professor Ronald Rohner of the University of Connecticut said:

> In the US, Great Britain and Europe, we have assumed for the last 300 years that all children need for normal healthy development is a loving relationship with their mother.
>
> And that dads are there as support for the mother and to support the family financially but are not required for the healthy development of children.
>
> But the belief is fundamentally wrong. We have to start getting away from that idea and realise the dad's influence is as great, and sometimes greater, than the mother's.[89]

Norman Wells, Director of the Family Education Trust, said that this study:

> underlines the importance of intact and stable families where both the father and the mother are committed to bringing up their children together.[90]

## 2.10    The Position of the Churches

The former Archbishop of Canterbury, Lord Carey, has observed that "the state does not 'own' the institution of marriage. Nor does the church." He adds that:

> The honourable estate of matrimony precedes both the state and the church, and neither of these institutions have the right to redefine it...[91]

---

[89] Quoted in the Daily Mail, 14 June 2012.
[90] Ibid.
[91] Daily Mail, 20 February 2012.

Although marriage is a universal institution thousands of years old, it also holds a distinct and unique place in Christian belief, and it therefore bears upon the lives of a large portion of the world's population. Much has been written about married life for those living out the Christian faith. The Church Fathers added much insight to the Church understanding of the spousal relationship and its connection to God. For the current purposes, we will briefly consider two positions: that of the Anglican and Roman Catholic understandings of marriage.

According to the Common Worship marriage service, which is derived from the Book of Common Prayer of 1662:

> The Bible teaches us that marriage is a gift of God in creation and a means of his grace, a holy mystery in which man and woman become one flesh. It is God's purpose that as husband and wife give themselves to each other in love throughout their lives, they shall be united in that love as Christ is united with his Church.

> Marriage is given that husband and wife may comfort and help each other, living faithfully together in need and in plenty, in sorrow and in joy. It is given that with delight and tenderness they may know each other in love and through the joy of their bodily union may strengthen the union of their hearts and lives. It is given as the foundation of family life in which children may be born and nurtured in accordance with God's will, to his praise and glory.

> In marriage husband and wife belong to one another and they begin a new life together in the community. It is a way of life that all should honour and it must not be undertaken carelessly, lightly or selfishly but reverently, responsibly and after serious thought.[92]

The above understanding of the marriage union is "seen" through a Christian lens. There are, however, basic components that define the marriage relationship, shared in by married couples throughout the world, irrespective of faith, or lack of faith. The husband and wife unit is the foundation of, and setting within which, any children conceived will be nurtured. There is also a public dimension to a married couple's life; it is not a private, ad hoc arrangement, hidden from communal knowledge and recognition.

One core source of authority, from which the universal Church has derived its understanding of marriage, is taken directly from Jesus who, quoting from Genesis in the Old Testament, states:

---

[92] Quoted in *A Response to the Government Equalities Office Consultation – "Equal Marriage" – from the Church of England*, (2012), p. 2.

But at the beginning of creation God 'made them male and female'. For this reason a man will leave his father and be united to his wife, and the two will become one flesh.' So they are no longer two, but one.[93]

Adultery, as a breach of the marriage vow, is taken seriously by the church, though there is always accommodation for forgiveness. The sin of adultery, stated explicitly in the Ten Commandments, was treated with equal gravity by Jesus, when he said:

> You have heard that it was said, 'Do not commit adultery.' But I tell you that anyone who looks at a woman lustfully has already committed adultery with her in his heart.[94]

What does the Roman Catholic Church teach about marriage? Over 2,000 years, much teaching and commentary on the sacrament of marriage has been written. According to the Catechism:

> By its very nature conjugal love requires the inviolable fidelity of the spouses. This is the consequence of the gift of themselves which they make to each other. Love seeks to be definitive; it cannot be an arrangement 'until further notice'. The 'intimate union of marriage, as a mutual giving of two persons, and the good of the children, demand total fidelity from the spouses and require an unbreakable union between them.'[95]

This position stands in sharp contrast to the view articulated in *The Transformation of Intimacy* by Lord Giddens. He describes a characteristic of modern relationships as expressing "plastic sexuality". The 'project of self' is realised in what he calls 'pure relationships' where sexual expression is unregulated by external standards and rules and lasts for as long as the parties to the relationship feel that they are receiving the desired level of satisfaction, "until further notice". In plastic sexuality, sexuality is separated from reproduction, while the means of reproduction via reproductive technologies has separated itself from institutional controls and norms that had previously stood untouched:

> [That which] holds the pure relationship together is the acceptance on the part of each partner, "until further notice", that each gains

---

[93] Mark 10: 6-8. (NIV version)
[94] Matthew 5: 27-28. (NIV version)
[95] *The Catechism of the Catholic Church*. (1994), p. 368

sufficient benefit from the relationship to make its continuance worthwhile.[96]

On the question of conjugal love, the Catholic Church further states:

> 'Conjugal love involves a totality, in which all the elements of the person enter – appeal of the body and instinct, power of feeling and affectivity, aspiration of the spirit and of will. It aims at a deeply personal unity, a unity that, beyond union in one flesh, leads to forming one heart and soul; it demands *indissolubility* and *faithfulness* in definitive mutual giving; and it is open to *fertility*...'[97]

It seems that some of those in the gay Christian world are open to and embrace a more flexible understanding and practice of monogamy. *Changing Attitude* (CA), the UK's premier LGBT (Lesbian, Gay, Bisexual and Transgender) organisation does not insist on the standard of sexual monogamy in same-sex relationships. In 2004 it stated:

> Thus while it is clear to us as LGBTs when we survey the gay scene, and indeed much of contemporary social life, that casual sex can often be addictive and destructive, we think it is important to remain open to the possibility that brief and loving sexual engagement between mature adults in special circumstances can be occasions of grace...The exploration of our sexual selves can be something which benefits from involvement with more than one person.[98]

Alongside this, CA recognises elsewhere[99] that like heterosexual couples, gays and lesbians also:

> commit...to partners in faithful, loving monogamous relationships. We also fall in exactly the same way as heterosexuals. Partners are sometimes unfaithful, and relationships can break down.[100]

The above statements are conveyed here so that a larger picture is provided of how same-sex relationships are also understood by those who believe that there

---

[96] Giddens (1992), p. 63.

[97] *The Catechism of the Catholic Church.* (1994), p. 368

[98] Quoted at: http://www.anglican-mainstream.net/2011/10/12/gay-marriage-hidden-implications-and-impact-3/

[99] See: *All God's Children: Lesbian and Gay People in the Anglican Church*: A brief guide to understanding the role and history of lesbian and gay people in the Anglican church.
http://changingattitude.org.uk/wp-content/uploads/2010/11/All-Gods-Children.pdf

[100] Ibid.

is no contradiction between theologically, biblically-based standards about sexual ethics and the morally relative values of modern lifestyles.[101]

## 2.11    The Equality Argument: Are there Unintended Consequences?

The notion of equality holds a long history that extends back to ancient times and draws on the disciplines of philosophy and theology. That there are varying notions of what constitutes the ideal of equality jars with what is sometimes popularly depicted as a black and white issue; namely, that there is implicitly one view of equality that all civilised nations must adhere to. Any position that differs from this orthodox view is viewed with immediate suspicion.

Although there are differing formulations of what constitutes "equality", a common version takes the form of treating people in similar situations in an equal manner. Treating persons in similar situations *differently,* without an objective and reasonable justification is, broadly speaking, taken to be 'discrimination'. Yet, there will be differing views as to how this general principle is applied to a wide spectrum of situations. We should clarify that underlying this whole debate is the presumption that all human beings are automatically of equal worth, irrespective of the lifestyle adopted or status. As noted earlier, confusion in this area can and does lead to the wrong conflation of "gay people" and "gay relationships".

William (now Lord) Rees-Mogg had this to say about civil partnerships and the law in general:

> Almost all law is concerned with discriminating between different cases that receive different treatment. Even the Civil Partnership Act is avowedly discriminatory. Same-sex couples gain substantial tax advantages, equal to those of a married couple. Members of the same family are not allowed to enter into civil partnerships with each other;

---

[101] In stark contradiction to the often repeated assertions that Jesus was not so much concerned with sexual ethics because his primary concern was with the poor, the evidence studied reveals a different story. See: John Nolland, *Sexual Ethics and the Jesus of the Gospels.* ANVIL, Vol. 26, No. 1, (2009). While it is true that the ministry of Jesus was not primarily centred on sexual ethics, he nevertheless openly advocated the standard of sexual monogamy while unambiguously condemning sexual activity outside of marriage. The Jewish culture to which he spoke would not have embraced any version of a same-sex relationship, although this historical given has been doubted by some writers. For what is the most thorough, authoritative and systematic treatment currently published on this topic and its related issues, see: Robert A. J. Gagnon, *The Bible and Homosexual Practice: Texts and Hermaneutics.* Nashville, Tennessee: Abingdon Press, (2001).

> nor are unmarried heterosexual couples. These seem to me to be unfair discriminations, but that is not the point. They undoubtedly are discriminatory and the exclusion of heterosexual couples is undoubtedly a discrimination based on sexual orientation. It is a matter of same sex, yes, but different sexes, no. [102]

Rees-Mogg's argument about family members being excluded was an often argued-for point by those who believed the new civil partnership law was not as fair as it was billed by the government of the day. One conclusion to be drawn here is that by only according same-sex couples the rights to enter civil partnerships, the government was evidently elevating the status of sexual relationships *above* all other relationships. So, two sisters who live together could not, upon the death of one of them, benefit from inheritance laws. Siblings are one of the legally prohibited relationships who can enter civil partnerships.

On the question of marriage, until perhaps 30 or so years ago, the proposition that allowing homosexuals to marry was an equality issue would have appeared ludicrous, nor would any judge or legal scholar have contemplated such a notion as reasonable, given the lack of fulfilment for conditions of eligibility. In itself this serves to highlight the distinction between varying types of relationship, both opposite and same sex, and the special status attaching to marriage as a socially recognised institution, providing the basic framework for family.

It has argued that the State should not stop people getting married unless there are good reasons, and "being gay" is not one of them. [103] This appears to contradict the argument commonly asserted that homosexuals and lesbians are not allowed to marry their own sex *because* of their sexual orientation. We will briefly consider questions connected to "sexual orientation" below, because this directly bears upon how we might understand and apply our concept of equality. In this discussion, we understand that what is deemed "sexual orientation" – compared with, for example, skin colour – does not merit being classified as a 'class' for the purposes of formulating and applying our notion of equality.

On the matter of equality and its relationship to sexual orientation, Home Secretary Theresa May said:

> For me, equality is about fairness: it's about equal treatment and equal opportunity. [104]

---

[102] The Times, 5 February 2007. "Adopt Change after 2000 years? Never!"
[103] Discussion at General Synod, York, July 2012.
[104] Stonewall Workplace Conference Speech, 18 March 2011.

On another occasion, she asked:

> Should two people who care deeply for each other, who love each other and who want to spend the rest of their lives together be allowed to marry? That is the essential question behind the debate over the Government's plans to extend civil marriage to same-sex couples.
>
> My answer is that marriage should be for everyone, regardless of their sexual orientation.[105]

In a statement that now appears to have become popular opinion, May clarified the role of the State in the domain of promoting equality:

> I don't believe the State should perpetuate discrimination and prejudice. I believe that in modern Britain we should seek to eliminate discrimination wherever we find it.[106]

If *all* adult-consenting relationships, not believed to involve harm, are of equal value in society's eyes – an idea that sits at the heart of the equality and diversity agenda – then there are some disturbing 'elephants in the room' that will bring embarrassment to all those in the public square who speak incessantly about equality – a view summed up by Gordon Brown, when he gave voice to the words of a new "injunction": "you can't legislate love".[107]

We ask, for example, why should two homosexual siblings, who profess love for one another, be denied the right to enter a civil partnership? Or, if same-sex marriage were introduced, why would they also be discriminated against by virtue of their sibling relationship? Society is silent about scenarios like these, even though it claims to be non-judgmental about sexual behaviour.

All too frequently we are reminded that all love is the same, so this invites the compelling question that if there are two adults (who are family members) who want the same rights as gay couples, on what moral or other grounds can the State possibly justify discrimination? Indeed, why do the gay lobby and its heterosexual "equality" supporters discriminate against such relationships? The short answer is that society still judges such relationships as taboo. But, on the basis of the proposition that all love is the same and should be given free

---

[105] The Times, 15 March 2012.

[106] The Times, 15 March 2012.

[107] Former Prime Minister, Gordon Brown stated this new modern injunction that "you can't legislate love". http://www.telegraph.co.uk/news/politics/gordon-brown/5725041/Gordon-Brown-says-You-cant-legislate-love.html?vm=r  (3 July 2009)

expression (when legally consenting), irrespective of the orientation, on what grounds of argument can incestuous sexual relationships be excluded?

In the case of close family members involving the opposite sex, discrimination can be justified on the ground that any offspring generated by such a relationship is at risk of genetically-based health risks. However, this problem of risks is *absent* in same-sex based relationships involving incest. The risks too would also be absent in an opposite-sex incestuous relationship where the female party is either beyond childbearing age, undertakes to use "safe" contraception, or alternatively, where she is infertile.

These cited scenarios are not mere speculation but are some of the actual consequences that flow from the beliefs about what ought to constitute our notion of "equality". While instances of incest have always been present in society, the pertinent question is: if the doctrine of equality popularly commended by our government and "equality" advocates is fundamentally flawed, our society ought to re-think and begin to question its beliefs about what is acceptable sexual behaviour.

## Questions of Labelling, Orientation and Welfare

### 2.12 (a)    Labelling and Orientation

While it is true, for example, that predominant homosexual attraction may exclude sufficient heterosexual interest for marriage to become a feasible option, this is not the whole story. Traditionally, people have married for a wealth of reasons, and some of these, without doubt, have been based less on 'attraction' and far more on the desire for social approval. Similarly some, experiencing sexual ambivalence, will nevertheless have married for entirely genuine reasons and found their lives immeasurably enriched.

What we do know now is that what is labelled as "sexual orientation" is far from black and white.[108] For example, men are known to actively engage in one-off same-sex acts, but do not necessarily feel the desire to replicate this with other males. Alternatively, some have deliberately engaged in specific same-sex sexual acts, while at the same time feeling repulsed by other sexual acts with the same sex. Many of these men can lead functional heterosexual lives - but in a limited dimension of experience, and their sexual outlet takes a different turn. Are these men homosexual? Or gay? Some gay apologists seem

---

[108] For a further examination of this topic, see: Stein, Edward. (1999). *The Mismeasure of Desire: The Science, Theory and Ethics of Sexual Orientation*. Oxford University Press.

inclined to describe such sexuality as "repressed homosexuality" but this claim is mere speculation.

Is such labelling determined by the sexual activities performed? If so, how frequent do these activities need to occur before the definition of "being homosexual" applies – as opposed to having merely performed same-sex acts on an ad hoc or one-off basis? Is it based on inner feelings, and if so, must these feelings be purely ones of arousal, or is an overall attraction to the same sex also required? Another question is whether the choice to label or not label someone as "homosexual" could actually be one of personal autonomy.

An important moral question is whether it is society with its collected beliefs, or an individual with his or her own beliefs and values, that determines how one is to be labelled. In fact, some such people, whose voice it is true is less heard in contemporary culture, choose not to identify with their same-sex sexual attractions, resolutely rejecting the label of being "gay". Current society finds this difficult to accept, rather like – though in a very different context – when it struggled to accept that people could actually perform homosexual acts!

That there are people who do not feel a need to identify with their sexual attractions contradicts the currently received wisdom that would argue such people are 'living in denial' and carry 'internalised homophobia'. But is human flourishing dependent on the performance of certain sexual acts? Is human identity not something tied up, at least in part, to personal autonomy and individual values about self? For many people, their sense of identity is connected to their own families and communities. Identity is understood in a diverse number of ways, given the many societies that make up our world. It is ironic that, on the one hand, our society boasts of its "diversity" credentials. Yet people holding views and values on matters of sexuality that are out of harmony with the 'new orthodoxy', are viewed with suspicion. It seems the only way society has learned to respond to such people is to explain away their philosophical or religious choices as 'internalised homophobia'. We do not believe such people are positively included in the "diversity" so often celebrated.

Is society the only qualified arbiter to decide?

The question of what constitutes 'sexual orientation' is far from being a straightforward proposition, and it is shallow and unhelpful to suppose that people either fit into one category or another, and thus need take on the label that society has created for them.

If experiences of sexual attraction defy, as they appear to do, compartmentalisation, it is erroneous to equate orientation with skin colour; as a given that one is born with – innate and immutable. To date, no scientific evidence has found a "gay gene". Neither has a genetic component been discovered that is shown to predispose people in their sexual attraction.

While there is no consensus among mental health practitioners as to what components lead to the development of same-sex attractions, some credible studies do provide evidence that specific sexual attractions are not experienced as fixed in everyone.[109] This fact must bear upon our formulation of equality as a concept, because if sexual orientation is not fixed, we are dealing with an 'inclination' rather than a fixed property, such as gender or skin colour.

Attempts are now made in courts of law to draw parallels between historic race discrimination, and gays being excluded from the "right" to marry. However, such comparisons are unjustified, because in cases of legal prohibition on the grounds of colour, the proposed union was not deemed to contravene any commonly defined legal principles constituting marriage but grounded rather in the contravention of national and State policies that forbade racial intermarriage.

Typically, mental health bodies reject the notion that people can change their sexual orientation. Put differently, the idea that an individual can make a lifestyle choice, rejecting the gay label, even though experiencing same-sex attractions, is denied. It would seem indeed that current politics genuflect uncritically to gay political sensitivities, deliberately downplaying the findings of case studies that show homosexual feelings lie within a spectrum and can change, in some cases giving way to heterosexual attractions.[110]

---

[109] In the study of lesbians, see Lisa M. Diamond: *Was it a phase? Young women's relinquishment of lesbian/bisexual identities over a 5-year period.* Journal of Personality and Social Psychology, 84 (2), 352-364 (2003). *A new view of lesbian subtypes: Stable versus fluidity trajectories over an 8-year period.* Psychology of Women Quarterly, 29 (2), 119-128 (2005). *Female bisexuality from adolescence to adulthood: Results from a 10-year longitudinal study.* Developmental Psychology, 44, 5-14 (2008). In the study of homosexuals, see the longitudinal study by 1) Jones, Stanton L and Yarhouse, Mark A. (2007), *Ex-Gays? A Longitudinal Study of Religiously Mediated Change in Sexual Orientation.* Illinois: IVP Academic, InterVarsityPress; 2) Jones, Stanton, L and Yarhouse, Mark, A. (2009), *Ex-Gays? An Extended Longitudinal Study of Attempted Religiously Mediated Change in Sexual Orientation.* Sexual Orientation and Faith Tradition Symposium, APA Convention. See also: Spitzer, Robert. *Can Some Gay Men and Lesbians Change Their Sexual Orientation? 200 Participants Reporting a Change from Homosexual to Heterosexual Orientation.* Archives of Sexual Behavior. Vol., 32, No. 5, October 2003, 403-417.

[110] Ibid., see especially the rigorous and longitudinal study by Jones and Yarhouse.

## 2.12 (b)   Welfare

Another highly relevant issue connected to this debate is that of welfare and health. Messages from those in authority try to depict homosexual practice as healthy. In fact, the Deputy Prime Minister described homosexual relationships as normal and harmless.[111] This echoes the position of the leading mental health bodies – but it leaves a conflict of messages in the public square.

Homosexual practice appears to have existed in most, if not all societies. The fact of a phenomena manifesting as a historical norm, only points to the fact of its presence. However, the factual historical dimension tells us nothing about whether this 'norm' *ought* to be treated legally as a healthy norm.

Medical studies plainly show the dangers of homosexual penetrative sex, although this fact is rarely mentioned today in public debate.[112] It should be noted that not all homosexuals practice penetrative sex. There is, however, a real risk of damage to the rectal lining, which is unable to withstand the same pressures as that of the vagina. There are therefore grave risks to health that go far beyond HIV transmission.[113]

---

[111]http://www.independent.co.uk/news/uk/politics/clegg-lays-down-law-to-cameron-on-gay-rights-1866116.html  (13 January 2010)

[112] For lay readers, see:  Diggs MD, John, R. (2002). *The Health Risks of Gay Sex*. The Corporate Resource Council. For more specialist medical publications, see: *Anal Cancer Incidence: Genital Warts, Anal Fissure or Fistula, Hemorrhoids, and Smoking*, (November 1989),  Holly, et al, Journal of the National Cancer Center Institute, (Vol. 81, No. 22); *Depressive Disorders and unprotected casual anal sex among Australian homosexually active men in primary care*, (2003), Rogers et al, British HIV Association (4, 271-275); *Physical Health Complaints Among Lesbians, Gay Men, and Bisexual and Homosexually Experienced Heterosexual Individuals: Results from the California Quality of Life Survey*, (November 2007), Cochran et al, American Journal of Public Health, (Vol. 97, No. 11); *Beyond Anal Sex: Sexual Practices Associated with HIV Risk Reduction among Men Who Have Sex with Men in Boston, Massachusetts*, (November 2009), Reisner et al. AIDS PATIENT CARE and STDs (Vol. 23, No. 7)

[113] Dr Jeffrey Satinover, distinguished psychiatrist, in his book, *Homosexuality and the Politics of Truth* explains that even when condoms are used, "anal intercourse is harmful primarily to the "receptive" partner. Because the rectal sphincter is designed to stretch only minimally, penile-anal thrusting can damage it severely. The introduction of larger items, as in the relatively common practice of "fisting," causes even worse damage. Thus gay males have a disproportionate incidence of acute rectal trauma as well as of rectal incontinence (the inability to control the passing of feces) and anal cancer." (p. 67). Of anal intercourse, Dr Satinover explains that whether "penile or otherwise, [it] traumatizes the soft tissues of the rectal lining. These tissues are meant to accommodate the relatively soft fecal mass as it is prepared for expulsion by the slow contractions of the bowel and are nowhere near as sturdy as vaginal tissue. As a consequence, the lining of the rectum is almost always traumatized to some degree by any act of anal intercourse." (p. 67). See bibliography.

Studies also abound which show a disproportionately high presence of depression, anxiety and other mental disorders in "men who have sex with men" (MSM), compared with what is found among heterosexuals.[114] The term MSM is typically used in much of the literature rather than "gay". Common interpretations attribute "internalised homophobia" – society's non-acceptance – as the cause of this pathology. This causal explanation is questionable; there is no science that supports this hypothesis. In fact, the *DSM Manual* (bible of diagnoses of mental disorders used by mental health practitioners) has no record of "internalised homophobia" as a specific mental health condition. It is noteworthy that in liberal countries like the Netherlands, the mental health of MSM appears not to have diminished, which brings into question many of the conventional opinions about homophobia.[115]

Of the 2010 statistics for HIV diagnosis, the Terence Higgins Trust (THT), the largest HIV and sexual health charity in the UK stated:

> 45% of new HIV diagnoses in 2010 were among men who have sex with men. Gay and bisexual men remain the group at highest risk of contracting HIV in the UK, making up 69% of HIV infections acquired sexually.[116]

HIV statistics for the previous year made up:

> 42% of new HIV diagnoses in 2009 were among men who have sex with men. Gay men remain the group at highest risk of contracting HIV in the UK, making up 67% of those acquiring the infection in this country.[117]

---

[114] See: *Is Sexual Orientation Related to Mental Health Problems and Suicidality in Young People?* (October 1999), Fergusson et al, Archives of General Psychiatry (56: 876-880); *Lifetime Prevalence of Suicide Symptoms and Affective Disorders Among Men Reporting Same-Sex Sexual Partners: Results from NHANES III*, (April 2000), Cochran et al, American Journal of Public Health (Vol. 90, No. 4); *Distress and Depression in Men Who Have Sex With Men: The Urban Men's Health Study* (February 2004), Mills et al, American Journal of Psychiatry (161: 2); *Gay/Lesbian sexual orientation increases risk for cigarette smoking and heavy drinking among members of a large Northern California health plan*, (October 2006), Gruskin, Elizabeth and Gordon, Nancy, BMC Public Health (6: 241); *A systematic review of mental disorder, suicide, and deliberate self harm in lesbian, gay and bisexual people*, (2008), King et al, BMC Psychiatry (8: 70).

[115] See for example: *Same-Sex Behavior and Psychiatric Disorders: Findings from the Netherlands Mental Health Survey and Incidence Study (NEMESIS)*, (January 2001), Sandfort et al, Archives of General Psychiarty (Vol. 58, No. 1);

[116] *HIV in the UK in 2010*, Bulletin, December 2011.

[117] *HIV in the UK in 2009*, Bulletin, November 2010.

There is plainly a disproportionate relationship between the high rates of HIV diagnoses among "gay men" and the fact that, as a group, they represent only a small section of the overall population.[118]  However, we believe it is more accurate to draw a link, not so much between "gay men" and medically adverse sexual activities involving the anus, but between these activities and all those persons who habitually perform such activities. Put differently, it is not the 'orientation' or the people that are the issue here, but specific acts that are high risk behaviours.

According to the US Centers for Disease Control and Prevention (CDC), which forms part of the Department of Health and Human Services, gay and bisexual men are "more severely affected by HIV than any other group in the United States."[119] The CDC acknowledges the hugely disproportionate relationship between the HIV statistics and the numbers of gay and bisexual men, and other men (MSM) who collectively make up approximately only 2% of the US population.[120]

In 2009, MSM made up 61% of new HIV infections in the US, while the same group accounted for 79% of infections among all newly infected men.[121] In 2010, of the estimated HIV diagnoses among all males of 13 years and above, MSM accounted for 78%. This estimate was based on data from 46 out of 50 states with long-term confidential, name-based reporting.[122]

The CDC recommends that sexually active MSM are tested for HIV once every 3-6 months.[123] It also recommends that the "most effective ways to prevent HIV and many other sexually transmitted infections" are to use condoms when such behaviours are practised, or contrary to the received wisdom, to "avoid anal sex".[124]

We should state that tolerance of a medically risky behaviour in society is a quite different proposition from that of exposing young people to messages seeking to affirm homosexual practice as a healthy behaviour. The identity of young people is at that stage in process of continuing development. Compare this with society's large and vigorous anti-smoking strategy, carried out through numerous health campaigns. The strategy is not generally interpreted

---

[118] *Just one in 100 tells researchers: I'm gay*, Ben Leapman, Daily Telegraph, 27 January 2008. These findings were the result of government research, and was known as the first of its kind.

[119] *HIV Among Gay and Bisexual Men*, May 2012, CDC, p. 1.
http://www.cdc.gov/hiv/topics/msm/pdf/msm.pdf

[120] Ibid., p. 1.

[121] Ibid., p. 1.

[122] Ibid., p. 1.

[123] Ibid., p. 2.

[124] Ibid., p. 2.

as an assault on smokers as human beings. Instead, the anti-smoking campaign is premised on the medical fact that smoking is bad for physical health and should therefore be actively discouraged. How infinitely more dangerous are the health risk behaviours advocated by some so-called sexual health providers?

David Cameron, when asked whether he agreed with Nick Clegg that homosexuality was "normal and harmless" replied with several points, saying:

> We do need good sex and relationship education. That education should teach people about equality and the sort of country we are – that we treat people the same whether they are straight or gay...It is important that ethos is embedded in our schooling.

He added:

> But should we teach children about relationships? Yes, we should. Should we teach them about consent? Yes, we should. Should we teach them about the importance of equality, whether you are heterosexual or homosexual? Yes, we should. Should we teach them about civil partnerships being the way of same-sex couples showing commitment just as married couples show commitment? Yes, we should.[125]

It ought to be a given that society should treat all people with equal and unconditional respect as persons, irrespective of their inclinations. However, in the second extract Cameron acknowledges that homosexual relationships must be promoted in schools because it is about commitment, of a comparable kind to the commitment of married couples.

In light of the medical concerns we raise here about homosexual practice, why should such medically risky behaviour be portrayed as healthy in schools and conveyed through the prism of equality? We do not know how Cameron would answer this question directly, but he is on record as stating something that we understand sums up the wider attitudes of fear that increasingly govern the wider debate. On the question of Section 28, the provision that banned councils from funding the promotion of homosexuality in schools, he said that this law was:

> something that a lot of people in this country find very offensive, and on that basis, it can't be a sensible thing to do.[126]

---

[125] www.guardian.co.uk/politics/2010/jan/28/david-cameron-gay-equality (28 January 2010)
[126] http://www.independent.co.uk/news/uk/politics/lets-talk-about-sex-johann-hari-grills-david-cameron-over-gay-rights-1888688.html (4 February 2010)

Evidently, it is the fear of causing offence that is shaping the response strategy mounted by a party once perceived as anti-gay. It reflects what may be observed more widely as a culture of fear of causing offence. The compelling question is: should the risk of causing offence *absolutely* outweigh the serious risks to health that might otherwise be mitigated

# 3

# THE LEGAL EVOLUTION ARGUMENT

## 3.1  Past Marriage Reform

Throughout the world, the laws and rules governing society have varied significantly over the course of time in both their specific content and *modus operandi*. This is true in everything ranging from the domain of criminal law and sentencing, to the large edifice of civil law. With this broad principle in mind, how do we apply this historical fact to the question of marriage as an institution, in the context of redefining marriage altogether?

Skelton and Flint appeal to a collection of examples of marriage reform that have unfolded in this country. They seek to argue that redefining marriage, so that same-sex couples are recognised as eligible parties to a marriage, is just another piece of marriage law reform that is part of an evolution of the institution. They state:

> In Western civilisation, marriage has been a vital building block of society for centuries. However, the nature of marriage has also changed considerably over time – it has evolved with society and has remained a pivotal part of it. Crucially, the state has acted to extend marriage to excluded groups three times in the past two centuries and the state also introduced marriage that was separate from religion almost two hundred years ago. The current law on marriage has therefore formed over centuries. [127]

In their appeal to some examples of marriage reform itself, the authors write:

> Civil marriages were introduced in 1836 in which a religious element was optional. Jews and Quakers were given the freedom to marry in the manner of their faith the previous year. Catholics were not included until later. This demonstrates historical precedent of the state

---

[127] Skelton, David and Flint, Robert. (2012), p.8.

intervening to help define marriage and intervening to incorporate groups who were previously excluded.[128]

In the first extract above, Skelton and Flint claim that the "nature of marriage has ... changed considerably over time – it has evolved with society." Examples of this change given in the second above excerpt highlight instances where the state had allowed three groups to marry on the terms of their own faith, which was formerly unlawful (Jews, Quakers and Catholics).

The enduring nature of marriage – which we set out in Chapter 2, is wrongly being conflated here with the question of specific ethnic and religious groups being given rightful access to this institution on their own religious terms. Prior to the respective legal reforms which discriminated against people because of their religion, the "one man, one woman" marriage model clearly remained intact. The legal reforms did not change the *nature* of marriage, as claimed by Skelton and Flint. Rather, they merely extended the legal right to marry, to a wider pool of men and women.

In the second extract, it is argued that the legal reforms pertaining to Jews, Quakers and Catholics "demonstrates historical precedent of the state intervening to help define marriage and intervening to incorporate groups who were previously excluded." The precedent in question was not about the state helping to "define marriage". Allowing the stated groups to marry in the manner of their faith did nothing to change the essential meaning of marriage. What it did was to allow those with different traditions and beliefs to have the right to enter the institution in line with their own faith. The evolution of marriage reforms had not altered the intrinsic meaning of marriage in any respect. The six essential conditions we examined earlier remained intact. While the respective religious traditions characterising the groups under our focus hold differing theological beliefs in relation to marriage, all recognise and share the six defining conditions.[129] They are: 1) one man and one woman; 2) procreative potential; 3) sexual exclusivity; 4) permanence; 5) mutual commitment; and 6) public recognition.

There is a real difference between the propositions of: 1) not recognising the rights of people on the basis of their ethnicity or religion to marry in ways that reflect their own faith; and 2) not recognising same-sex couples being *able* to marry under any circumstances due to ineligibility. In the first case, the groups excluded were by reason of their respective religious

---

[128] Ibid., p. 9.

[129] In terms of recent changes in thinking, one exception here is that of the Quakers, who have embraced the same-sex marriage proposition.

approaches to marriage. They were not excluded on the basis that they failed to satisfy the basic eligibility test of marriage, namely being an unmarried man and woman of legal age. Rather the fact of their exclusion rested on unfair discrimination.

The authors argue that while the institution of marriage has "changed and evolved over time" by incorporating groups like Jews, Quakers and Catholics, it has not lost its "unique character".[130] We understand this fact of uniqueness can only be a reference to the union of one man and one woman. By devising new terms of what constitutes a marriage, namely recognising that two men or two women can be "married", the uniqueness of the marriage institution is immediately lost.

Skelton and Flint also point out that civil marriages were introduced in 1836, when the religious element became optional. In terms of the intrinsic conditions which constitute a marriage, the religious or secular character of the ceremony does not negate or diminish the basic, foundational six components of marriage, as recognised above. Therefore, we reject the idea that the introduction of civil marriage can add anything meaningful to the arguments used in support of same-sex marriage.

The authors argue that a number of other legal reforms to marriage are further examples demonstrating State intervention in the evolution of marriage as a legal institution. For example, the 1857 Divorce and Matrimonial Causes Act "gave, for the first time, the common law courts, not religious courts or an Act of Parliament, marital jurisdiction."[131] For legal purposes, this evolution was a legal reform of those instruments of state, in respect of who held legal jurisdiction on issues connected to marriage. But the administrative aspect of jurisdiction is wholly different in kind to the legal definition of what can and cannot constitute a marriage.

Skelton and Flint also appeal to legal reform, in which "parameters" were established as to where and when a marriage could legally be held.[132] That the state intervened in these matters reveals but more instances of legal changes to the *administration* of marriage ceremonies. As acknowledged earlier, throughout history there have been many customs governing the marriage relationship. There have also been varying means by which public recognition of marriage has been made. However, the administrative dimensions of marriage ceremonies are merely secondary or extrinsic to those intrinsic and unchanging features that define marriage in its essential nature.

---

[130] Ibid., p. 34.
[131] Ibid., p. 10.
[132] Ibid., p. 11.

## 3.2    Current International Developments

Since 2001 when the Netherlands became the first country to introduce same-sex marriage, there have been a further ten countries that have followed suit. These are: Argentina, Belgium, Canada, Denmark, Iceland, Norway, Portugal, South Africa, Spain and Sweden. Same-sex marriage is provided for in Mexico City and is also recognised throughout Mexico. [133]

Some countries have introduced civil unions,[134] as opposed to marriage, for same-sex couples as well as bestowing some legal rights that typically go with the married status of male-female couples.

The US Defense of Marriage Act of 1996 was passed by the Clinton administration which provided that where individual states in the Union legislate for same-sex marriage, other states are not legally bound to recognise these contracts. This federal law remains in place.

Seven US states, as well as Washington DC, have introduced marriage for same-sex couples. Polls seeking to discover public opinion on this matter vary. However, to date, thirty-one states have made their democratic voice heard through referendums, in which the redefinition of marriage was rejected. In spite of this public solidarity of opinion, President Obama has now come out in support of gay marriage. [135]

In March 2012, a referendum in Slovenia rejected a family law provision that would have allowed same-sex couples to adopt children in some cases. [136] This is despite the fact that same-sex relationships have qualified for official recognition since 2006.

In September 2012, the Australian House of Representatives rejected a bill that would have legalised same-sex marriage. [137] The proposal was put separately before the Senate and was likewise rejected. [138]

---

[133] See: *Equal Civil Marriage: A Consultation*, Annex A.
[134] Full a full list of countries which provide same-sex unions see: Annex A of *Equal Civil Marriage: A Consultation*.
[135] The Times, 10 May 2012.
[136] http://www.independent.co.uk/news/world/europe/slovenians-reject-gay-adoption-law-in-referendum-7585060.html   (26 March 2012)
http://www.pinknews.co.uk/2012/03/26/gay-adoption-law-is-rejected-inslovenian-referendum/
(26 March 2012)
[137] http://www.bbc.co.uk/news/world-asia-19645307  (19 September 2012)
[138]http://www.theaustralian.com.au/news/breaking-news/oppn-whip-dusts-off-civil-partnership-bill/story-fn3dxiwe-1226477754881  (20 September 2012)

Given the support for same-sex marriage that exists in some quarters, one view taken seems to be 'if everyone else is doing it, we must follow'. This principle that seems to pay special regard to what appears to be the latest social trends, may be understood in the following way:

> When it comes to living arrangements, it is now usual for a trend or an increase along any dimension to be taken for a norm or an ideal. An underlying logic seems to dictate that the way things are going must be right simply because that is how they are going, and so, therefore, it must be embraced and furthered. Often incorporated into this response is the assumption that a trend not only signifies an overwhelming preference is already a majority or even a universal behaviour.[139]

The UK government is already using its global influence to ensure that countries around the world recognise same-sex relationships. This plan is clarified in the government's consultation on same-sex marriage:

> The Government would continue working to increase international recognition of same-sex relationships whether that was civil partnerships or civil marriages for same-sex couples.[140]

According to American law professor, James D. Wilets, who advocates same-sex marriage:

> Law is a culturally specific expression of the traditions and norms of a particular society.[141]

Evidently, the British government's intention to introduce same-sex marriage in England and Wales is not the end of the matter. Its ultimate strategy is clearly global, so that all other countries, irrespective of their cherished and well-founded beliefs, are deemed to be 'backward'[142] if they reject same-sex

---

http://www.theaustralian.com.au/news/breaking-news/gay-marriage-bill-defeated-in-senate/story-fn3dxiwe-1226478275106 (20 September 2012)

[139] Morgan, Patricia. (2007), p. 17. The context within which this quoted extract was originally applied by the author was to the fragmentation of households and the decline of marriage.

[140] *Equal Civil Marriage: A Consultation*, p. 16.

[141] Wardle et al, Chapter 11, "The Inexorable Momentum Toward National and International Recognition of Same-Sex Relationships: An International, Comparative, Historical, and Cross-Cultural Perspective."

[142] As one illustration of this view, Francis Maude, Conservative MP who is described as his party's "arch-moderniser", said of his party: "If we are seen as being defined by backward-looking social attitudes we will be seen as unacceptable and unelectable." Daily Mail, 7 March 2012.

relationships and same-sex marriage. The former Equalities Minister announced that Britain needs to be a "world leader" on the issue of gay rights.[143] Clearly, this approach demonstrates a lack of real sensitivity for the specific traditions and norms of other societies. Even though all the world's religions reject the practice of same-sex relationships - let alone the concept of same-sex marriage – the UK government believes it knows better and holds the moral right to negatively judge those whose beliefs differs from their own.

Where a government seeks to challenge – through whatever means – other cultures in respect of its definition of marriage and what is understood as normative (healthy) relationships, the test of genuine respect for the beliefs, norms and cultural and religious traditions of other countries fails. It is not the role of governments (democratic or otherwise) to decide that it holds the moral and legal right to devise a new meaning for the institution of marriage.

## 3.3    Creating Legal Fiction or Fact?

What can be said of countries in which same-sex marriage has already been introduced? Or, in the case of the UK,[144] in view of the case argued for in this study, how is same-sex marriage to be viewed, once it is legal?

We believe the concept of legal fiction would apply, specifically meaning that while same-sex marriage can exist in law, the eligibility tests we have examined would nevertheless be absent. A legal fiction indicates when something is legal on paper but its meaning is not intelligible enough to point to anything that accords with reality.[145]

---

[143] Daily Mail, 17 September 2011.
[144] The Scottish Executive also plans to bring in legislation for same-sex marriage.
[145] A bizarre case of a legal fiction is that of a Spanish woman from Galicia, who holds the papers registering her as the owner of the Sun. Her local notary public declares her to be the "owner of the Sun, a star of spectral type G2, located in the centre of the solar system, located at an average distance from Earth of about 149, 000, 000 kilometres". According to reports, an international agreement claims that countries cannot claim ownership of a planet or star but nothing is said with regard to individuals. The woman plans to charge a fee to anyone who uses the Sun yet she has yet to announce how she intends to implement the charge. See: http://www.dailymail.co.uk/news/article-1333776/Spanish-woman-Angeles-Duran-claims-owns-sun--plans-start-charging-ALL-users.html (29 November 2010); http://news.nationalpost.com/2010/11/29/spanish-woman-claims-to-own-the-sun/ (29 November 2010).

# 4

## THE SLIPPERY SLOPE ARGUMENT

### 4.1    Could Churches be Coerced to Perform Gay Marriage?

Concerns especially from the Church of England and Roman Catholic Church have arisen about the long-term consequences of gay marriage being legalised. The argument is: if same-sex couples can marry in civil ceremonies, the demands of equality law will ultimately mean that those religious establishments with marriage licences will be legally required to conduct same-sex marriages. Another point that has been argued is that we cannot, as a country, have two legal jurisdictions, each of which does not recognise the other.

The Coalition government has offered assurances that gay marriage will only be legal in civil law. It is not that churches will be under pressure to conduct gay weddings, however, but rather, to do so will be illegal.[146] As noted in the introduction, it was announced that the government will ensure that the relevant legal safeguards are in place so that religious establishments cannot be challenged legally on grounds of equality law. In light of influential legal opinions, we consider the view that undermines the government's official position. We also consider how there is some precedent which places the churches at risk of future coercion to perform same-sex marriages against their beliefs.

In a recent European Court of Human Rights (ECHR) case,[147] consideration was given to whether there was a right to same-sex marriage. The ECHR decided there was no such right. The court, however, quoted a resolution by the Parliamentary Assembly of the Council of Europe which said that where same-sex marriage is legalised, the State will be placed under an obligation to "ensure that rights and obligations [of same-sex couples] are equivalent to those of heterosexual couples in a similar situation." We acknowledge that the quoted resolution is not binding. However, by appealing to this resolution, it at once has the potential to raise the stakes of how the same-sex marriage debate is legally treated. A new threshold is potentially created – alongside the 'rush' to

---

[146] *Equal Civil Marriage: A Consultation*. Para., 1.7
[147] Gas and Dubois v France, 2012 (no. 25951/07)

bring gay marriage into other countries – so that this legal opinion can influence future jurisprudence.

The European Convention on Human Rights states that discrimination is prohibited (Article 14). Discrimination is broadly taken to refer to persons who, in similar situations, are treated differently without a justification that is objective and reasonable. On the basis of this principle, if civil same-sex marriage is made lawful, the government will not be able to easily maintain that there is a reasonable justification for only certain couples to marry in a religious establishment.

According to Neil Addison QC, senior barrister and religious liberty expert, if same-sex marriage is legalised, the ECHR stance, together with the Ladele judgement, means that the government view is at odds with the legal position. In *Ladele v Islington Council* [2009] EWCA Civ 1357, the Court of Appeal held that Ladele's view of marriage, namely, "the orthodox Christian view that marriage is the union of one man and one woman for life" was not a core part of her religion". However, in 2.10, we showed how Christian belief definitively includes this "orthodox" view of marriage. Addison concludes:

> The combined effect of the European Court decision and the Ladele decision seems to be clear. If same-sex marriage is legalised in the UK then religious same-sex marriage will have to be legalised also. Churches which perform heterosexual marriages will have to be willing to perform same-sex marriages and they will have no legal grounds to resist since the (secular) Courts have determined that the "Orthodox Christian view of Marriage" is not a "Core" part of Christian belief.[148]

He further states that the Church of England, as the established church, is under a legal obligation to marry all eligible persons in England and Wales. Even if there were a law that permits but does not force churches to host same-sex weddings, therefore, he believes the UK government could be in breach of the European human rights law.[149]

According to the Church of England Submission to the Government Equalities Office, introducing same-sex marriage would:

> alter the intrinsic nature of marriage as the union of a man and a woman as enshrined in human institutions throughout history.[150]

---

[148] http://religionlaw.blogspot.co.uk/ (17 April 2012)

[149] http://www.c4m.org.uk/downloads/legalopinionsummary.pdf

[150] *A Response to the Government Equalities Office Consultation* (2012), p. 1.

The Church of England warns that:

> The consultation paper wrongly implies that there are two categories of marriage, "civil" and "religious". This is to mistake the wedding ceremony for the institution of marriage. The assertion that "religious marriage" will be unaffected by the proposals is therefore untrue, since fundamentally changing the State's understanding of marriage means that the nature of marriages solemnized in churches and other places of worship would also be changed.
>
> To remove the concept of gender from marriage while leaving it in place for civil partnerships is unlikely to prove legally sustainable. It is unlikely to prove politically sustainable to prevent same sex weddings in places of worship given that civil partnerships can already be registered there where the relevant religious authority consents. And there have to be serious doubts whether the proffered legal protection for churches and faiths from discrimination claims would prove durable. For each of these reasons we believe, therefore, this consultation exercise to be flawed, conceptually and legally.[151]

Skelton and Flint in their case of "equal marriage", object to religious establishments being forced against their will to perform same-sex weddings. They argue:

> such a decision being made by the European Court of Human Rights or a similar court at UK level would represent an unnecessary act of judicial activism and an incursion of unelected judges into the realm of law making. Judges should not be replacing democratically accountable politicians as lawmakers in this sphere.[152]

Skelton and Flint's opposition to "judicial activism" is a position that would attract widespread support in theory. But in view of the *Ladele* case, and arguably in other cases, judges have exceeded the customary remit of their functions. For example, the orthodox Christian view of marriage undoubtedly occupies a *central* part in Christian belief. It is therefore disturbing that a judge can, as part of his decision, give judgment that declares it *not* to be a "core" component. As noted in Chapter 2 (section X), the role and meaning of marriage are not extrinsic or secondary to Christian belief, but integral to it.

It is true that judges cannot "make" law but only interpret existing law. However, senior courts must have regard to European jurisprudence made by the European Union. Directives produced by the EU, though of a different

---

[151] Ibid., p. 1.
[152] Skelton and Flint, p. 37.

jurisdiction from the ECHR, often have direct legal effect on member states. It is therefore possible, in theory, that English judges, in deference to our EU legal obligations, would override Westminster legislation that was found to be incompatible. Although this is not currently relevant, the main point here is that Westminster legislation is not totally independent, in that it is *not* immune from EU law.

In June 2012, Danish legislators introduced civil marriage for same-sex couples, as well as religious marriage, which takes effect in the state Lutheran Church, and other churches where the rules are permitting.[153] It is reported that polls suggest between one-third and half of the Lutheran Church's priests are unwilling to officiate at same-sex ceremonies.[154] Although the Lutheran Church must now provide weddings for same-sex couples, where clergy refuse, the Bishop must find another celebrant.[155] It is unclear what happens if a Bishop refuses to comply.

Denmark was the first country to introduce same-sex civil unions in 1989. This was followed in 1997 with same-sex couples being allowed to receive blessings in churches.

It is sometimes argued that because the Church of England already allows divorcees to remarry, with dissenting clergy allowed to refuse on grounds of conscience, same-sex marriage may likewise be accommodated by the Church, with non-complaint clergy being granted exemptions. This argument draws upon two patently non-comparable issues. Lord Carey clarifies the position:

> divorcees are not a grouping with the characteristics of a protected minority under human rights legislation. Clergy can refuse to remarry divorcees according to their conscience, with no possibility of discrimination claims being made under equality laws.[156]

The issue of tolerance is partly what is at issue in this area of the debate. The government, together with those of other parties, all currently agree that the churches should not be coerced to conduct same-sex marriage. However, we ask how this position sits alongside other legal issues flowing from both previous legislation and current messages from the government?

One 'test case', to be considered is that of the effect of the Sexual Orientation Regulations which, among various things, effectively ended the freedom of

---

[153] http://www.reuters.com/article/2012/06/08/us-denmark-homosexuals-marriage-idUSBRE8570UT20120608 (8 June 2012)
[154] Ibid.
[155] "A threat to the bonds of Church and state", Lord Carey, 13 June 2012, Daily Telegraph.
[156] Ibid.

adoption agencies affiliated to the Roman Catholic Church to continue providing services in accordance with their beliefs. The new law meant that adoption agencies had to consider providing adoption services to same-sex couples. The incompatibility of this new equality law with the Catholic Church's values of traditional family life, meant that they had one of two options. Either they could comply with the legislation and effectively sever their links to the Church. Or they could maintain their links to the Church and face legal action. The government of the day was uncompromising, believing that it was promoting fairness. But it placed its specific notion of, and belief in, its concept of equality *above* all other competing perspectives. We understand that although the current government desires to be perceived as tolerant in this area, it is not evident that this promised accommodation will be realised if same-sex civil marriage is legalised. Certainly, they have not demonstrated any willingness to support adoption agencies facing similar challenge.

David Cameron, shortly before he became Prime Minister stated decisively with regard to gay rights:

> the Church has to do some of the things that the Conservative Party has been through...recognising that full equality is a bottom-line, full essential.[157]

## 4.2 Could Gay Marriage Lead to Recognition of Poly Relationships and Plural Marriage?

Some traditional marriage advocates argue that if we introduce same-sex marriage, then this can potentially lead to polygamy being accepted. We consider some of the strong arguments that could be used in support of this claim.

Increasingly, advocates and practitioners of poly relationships believe they are also denied their rights to the same legal protections and benefits accorded to married couples. Polygamous relationships involve one man and at least two or more women. Polyamorous relationships involve any numerical combination of homosexual, heterosexual or bisexual persons. Dr Meg Barker, Open University psychologist, who has studied people who are in polyamorous relationships, points out that "Polyamory contests the ideal of the monogamous relationship..."[158] She writes:

---

[157] http://www.independent.co.uk/news/uk/politics/lets-talk-about-sex-johann-hari-grills-david-cameron-over-gay-rights-1888688.html  (4 February 2010)
[158] Barker (2004).

Common polyamorous set-ups include people having one or two 'primary' partners and other 'secondary' ones, triads (where three people are involved with each other), and quads (e.g. two couples being involved with each other). Some polyamorous people live together in families or tribes, some have 'polyfidelity' within their group and others are 'open'...[159]

One of the participants in Barker's study of polyamorous relationships said:

> To me polygamy is much simpler than Western conventional monogamy...[monogamy] is all very contradictory and cruel.[160]

Another observed that "Polygamy really is an extended family..."[161] On the comparison with monogamous relationships, another participant in the study said:

> I don't think it's vastly different to monogamous relationships. Romantic relationships are always about the same kinds of things: fun, friendship, sex.[162]

We understand that the rationale that is now used to justify social and legal recognition of poly relationships is essentially the same as those arguments made in support of same-sex marriage. We shall consider what factors are typically used in support of same-sex unions or same-sex marriage, highlighting the point that these factors are similarly advocated by practitioners of poly relationships.

## 4.2.1  Lifting the Legal Age of Consent

Persons who are party to a relationship must have reached the legal age of consent, which is the age at which the law presumes a person is adult enough to agree to sexual activity. Long before the gay marriage proposition came to the fore, gay liberationists were fighting to have the law changed so as to decriminalise same-sex activity – achieved first for adults of 21 years and above, followed by a further lowering of consent to the age of 18, and then to 16.

A relationship can be legal in this sense of consent, but not widely recognised socially. In the case of poly practitioners, while there may

---

[159] Ibid.
[160] Ibid.
[161] Ibid.
[162] Ibid.

be instances where some do not comply with the legal age of consent, to avoid legal censure advocates need merely comply with consent laws.

## 4.2.2 The 'slippery slope', from Taboo through Tolerance to Normalisation

With the progressive liberalisation of same-sex consent laws, the move to normalising homosexual behaviour grew from something held as taboo, to attracting gradual social tolerance, followed by acceptance of parity between same-sex and heterosexual relationships.

In 1967, the Earl of Arran, House of Lords' sponsor of Leo Abse's Commons bill that decriminalised homosexual acts said:

> This is no occasion for jubilation; certainly not for celebration. Any form of ostentatious behaviour; now or in the future, any form of public flaunting, would be utterly distasteful and would, I believe, make the sponsors of the Bill regret that they have done what they have done. Homosexuals must continue to remember that while there may be nothing bad in being a homosexual, there is certainly nothing good. Lest the opponents of the Bill think that a new freedom, a new privileged class, has been created...[163]

Although 1960s liberals, like the Earl of Arran, sought to free practising homosexual men from prosecution, it is clear from these comments that there was never any intention to create a new "privileged class", with special and unique rights favoured above those of others. As noted in the examples of the previous section, however, a body of burgeoning precedents demonstrates that the gay worldview is today being accorded disproportionate weight, going far beyond the intentions of those early reforming parliamentarians.

While we are not advocating the re-criminalisation of homosexual acts, there are parallels between what some see as the anticipated normalisation of poly relationships, and the normalisation of homosexual relationships, already seen. This is summed up John Ince, lawyer and spokesperson for the *Canadian Polyamory Advocacy Association*:

---

[163] Hansard, House of Lords debate, Sexual Offences (No. 2) Bill, 21 July 1967, Vol., 285 cc 522-6.

Gay history shows that liberation comes in steps. First gay relationships had to be accepted as legitimate and non-criminal. Once that occurred, then gay marriage followed. I think our normalization will follow the same course.[164]

One British MP, reflecting a consensus of growing unease, asked:

My overriding concern is that if we do indeed as a Parliament change legislation to allow same-sex marriage now, then what will our successors be discussing and have to legislate for in the future? Polygamy? Three-way relationships? Who knows what else?[165]

We should remember that the concept of "gay marriage" was not just beyond the contemplation of parliament in the 1960s, but would have been entirely foreign to the public imagination. As for poly relationships gaining social legitimacy and even some legal recognition, this cannot be ruled out. Reforms can have unintended consequences, at least as judged in hindsight.

## 4.2.3 Consent of the Parties

Alongside the legal age of consent being satisfied, persons must give their personal consent to both a relationship and any sexual acts performed within it.

In the case of polygamous relationships, critics argue that women are not accorded equal respect. This problem is addressed further below.

## 4.2.4 'Love and Commitment'

Love and commitment are the two necessary factors commonly cited by same-sex marriage advocates to justify allowing same-sex couples to marry. If love and commitment are the essential components supporting the case for same-sex marriage, then why reject those whose love and commitment are merely expressed to more people? Put simply, the argument largely rests on recognising the autonomous

---

[164] http://polyinthemedia.blogspot.co.uk/2011/11/canada-polygamy-ruling-win-loss-or-draw.html

[165] http://craigwhittakermp.wordpress.com/2012/10/01/talking-politics-halifax-courier-same-sex-marriage/ (8 May 2012)

decisions of people who choose to form a committed, group-based, sexual relationship.

## 4.2.5 The Equality Argument

Skelton and Flint argue against the 'slippery slope' thesis:

> As far as equality for gay and lesbian people is concerned, introducing equal marriage will almost be the final destination or the ultimate goal, rather than the beginning of a slippery slope.[166]

From the perspective of poly practitioners and their advocates, this argument is flawed because it ignores their perceived rights for legitimacy and equality. It may even be considered as indirectly promoting "polyphobia". It is disingenuous of gay activists and their "equality" supporters to claim to be "inclusive" and affirming of "diversity", while they are quick to distance themselves from any associations with other taboo "sexualities". This is perhaps one of the biggest 'elephants in the room' in this wider debate.

One writer in the Huffington Post describes the problem this way:

> ...if LGBTQ[167] activists continue to say that relationships are really about committing to the people we love regardless of race, gender, creed, etc., then maybe society should allow us to commit to the *people* (plural) we love. Note the assumption here; I believe it is, in fact, possible for some people to love more than one person.[168]

She further states:

> By distancing themselves and trying to divorce their struggle from the struggle of the poly/NM [non-monogamous] community, LGBTQ progressives end up throwing another sexual minority – indeed a minority within their own minority – under the bus...[169]

---

[166] Skelton and Flint (2012), p. 42.
[167] Lesbian, Gay, Bisexual, Transgender and Questioning.
[168] "Poly-Baiting: Why We Need a More Inclusive LGBT Movement", Vivienne Chen, 20 March 2012. See: http://www.huffingtonpost.com/vivienne-chen/gay-marriage-polyamory_b_1367260.html
[169] Ibid.

In the gay rights arena, one general argument underpinning equality is that because of the diverse ways in which people express love for one another, exercising moral disapproval is discriminatory, and thus undermines equality. The specific doctrinal version of equality promoted by gay activists and their heterosexual supporters effectively means that it is treated as the 'first principle' to which every value and belief must defer. From the poly perspective, the only principle that counts is this: if all relationships are truly equal in value, then why should only homosexuals and heterosexuals be included?

Some advocates, who support same-sex marriage, reject polygamy because it is deemed to promote exploitation and abuse of women. But others reject this presumption, as seen through the political and historical prism of oppression, arguing that poly practitioners believe they are freely choosing their lifestyle. They argue it is not for others to "judge" their personal choices, which hold no legitimate parallels with the historical oppression of women.

John Ince, an intervener in the British Columbia Supreme Court case (BC case), which failed to accord legal recognition to religious polygamous marriages, similarly rejects this presumption of oppression. His group filed written affidavits purportedly showing that there were happy polyamorous families across Canada, where partners were equal, and resources and duties for childcare were shared.[170] Of the lawmakers of the 1890s who legislated against polygamy, Ince argues against "patriarchal polygamy":

> They [lawmakers of the 1890s] could not anticipate the development of the post-modern institution of polyamory.[171]

Ince, unlike the Mormons who were arguing for polygamous rights in the BC case, has argued that there are non-religious polyamorists whose relationships do not equate with the non-egalitarian nature of the Mormon relationships cited in the case.[172]

There appears to be a direct parallel between Ince's position and a contemporary argument mounted by gay apologists. For example, some gay writers argue that the Bible writers who condemned homosexual acts had no concept of the loving same-sex relationships to which our modern world has now become accustomed. In other

---

[170] Reported in the Canadian Press, 14 April 2011. See:
http://www.cbc.ca/news/canada/british-columbia/story/2011/04/14/bc-polygamy-hearing-polyamorists.html
[171] Ibid.
[172] Ibid.

words, the Bible writers were not really condemning same-sex relationships, but rather, were condemning other illegitimate contexts for same-sex sexual activity, such as male prostitution. This is a large topic that opens up an area that goes beyond this current enquiry. But it suffices to say that Ince argues for a model of poly relationship that is not the kind that reflects the often cited instances where women are oppressed by men in polygamous – or by extension – in polyamoros relationships.

A Guardian writer who believes three or more people should be allowed to marry argues:

> This is not about the advocacy of patriarchal polygamy that regards wives as unequal to, or property of, their husbands. But if three, or four, or 17 people want to marry each other simultaneously and equally, why should they not be granted the same status as two people who want to become a legal family?[173]

## 4.2.6   The "do not judge" Injunction

Our pluralist society is influenced by what might be described as a quasi-moral injunction: "do not judge". In reality, our society is ready to judge a whole range of moral issues which invoke questions of "right" and "wrong". From questions about Fair Trade practices, to how the banking sector might be regulated, there are many instances where, as a society, we are willing to make moral judgments, and we are not morally reprimanded for exercising such rights. However, in the case of sexual choices in behaviour, this area has in recent decades become ring-fenced from moral scrutiny, in spite of the fact that there are numerous adverse consequences flowing from irresponsible sexual behaviour.

The underlying philosophy that appears to drive contemporary attitudes about sex seems to be that individuals act from their personal, autonomous choices. This freedom cannot, it is claimed, be morally questioned by others. Advocates of same-sex marriage cannot hold their position with any integrity if they "judge" that those in poly relationships are "wrong" in wanting to share in the benefits provided by legally recognised unions.

---

[173]   http://www.guardian.co.uk/commentisfree/2012/aug/30/three-people-get-married-thruple   (30 August 2012)

## 4.2.7   The Identity Argument

This narrative takes the form of "this is who I am". While the experience of homosexual feelings and attractions are very real for some people, we understand that the concept of "being gay" is a cultural construct that should be distinguished from performing specific sexual acts.

Historically, the "gay" concept grew out of a culture in which homosexuals felt they had no group to which they felt they belonged. In trying to affirm their sense of self and belonging, a socio-political identity of solidarity developed, which measured 'identity' according to sexual attractions and feelings. Even in Ancient Greece, it appears that there was no corresponding concept of a "homosexual" or "being gay". In his influential book, *Greek Homosexuality*, Sir Kenneth Dover points out that in the language of Ancient Greece, there were no nouns which existed corresponding to the English nouns of 'a homosexual' and 'a heterosexual'.[174]

The voices of poly advocates and practitioners are now being heard more regularly in mainstream academia, the media and the legal world.

Ann Tweedy, law professor, writing in the *Cincinnati Law Review*, studies the possibility of amending US state statutory definitions of sexual orientation for several reasons, including:

> the Supreme Court has not yet affirmatively espoused the view that discrimination based on sexual orientation is subject to heightened scrutiny under the Equal Protection Clause...[175]

Placing this in the larger context, she explains:

> Until sexual orientation is explicitly granted such heightened scrutiny, expanding definitions of sexual orientation to include other types of preferences is likely to result in little, if any, gain in the equal protection context for these newly added groups.[176]

---

[174] Dover (1989), p. 1.
[175] Tweedy (2011), p. 1462.
[176] Ibid., p. pp. 1461-1462.

On the question of polyamorists suffering discrimination, Tweedy imports a social justice argument that has been frequently used in the gay rights narrative:

> to the extent that polyamorists want legal protection, an issue that needs further investigation, it would be a beneficial move in terms of social justice to add polygamy to definitions of sexual orientation and thereby protect a societally disfavoured group from discrimination.[177]

Can polyamory be regarded as a "sexual orientation"? Tweedy believes there are "shared attributes" between polyamory and how sexual orientation has been understood:

> Because polyamory appears to be at least moderately embedded as an identity, [and] because polyamorists face considerable discrimination...anti-discrimination protections for polyamorists are warranted. Moreover, polyamory shares some of the important attributes of sexual orientation as traditionally understood, so it makes conceptual sense for polyamory to be viewed as part of sexual orientation.[178]

## 4.2.8 Voices within the Media

The media now appears to be comfortable in addressing issues of poly unions.

In 2011, heterosexual and bisexual polys 'came out' on ITV's *This Morning*.[179] In 2012, a writer in the *Guardian* considered the question: "If marriage is redefined once, [if same-sex marriage is legalised] what is to stop it being redefined to allow polygamy?"[180]

As for the perceived benefits to be enjoyed by children raised in polygamous unions, the journalist argues:

> What's wrong with polygamy? It seems to be that a child brought up by three loving parents would have some quite big economic

---

[177] Ibid., pp. 1514-1515.
[178] Ibid., p. 1514.
[179] 25 August 2011.
[180] http://www.guardian.co.uk/science/the-lay-scientist/2012/feb/20/1 (20 February 2012)

advantages, and humans have cooperated in child-rearing since the year dot.[181]

There is certainly a *prima facie* logic to the proposition that children born to polygamous households would be the beneficiaries of potentially larger economic gains. However, this surface argument obscures the fact that there can only be two natural parents who produce a child. Therefore, a third or fourth "parent" who happens to be a member of a polygamous set-up would not be expected to offer the same level of parenting resources.

The *Independent* ran a feature entitled: *Modern Lovers: The 'sexual body warriors' and pioneers transforming 21st-century relationships.*[182] One polyamorous English family is described in the following way:

> DK Green, 45, and his wives, Rachel Green, 49, and Luisa Green, 47 – affectionately dubbed the "tripod" – have lived together for more than a decade in a committed polyamorous relationship. They have raised three children and, like most other married couples, they share one bed – albeit 7ft in size...[183]

DK Green, biologically a woman, and self-defined "daddy of the house", "married" his two wives in a pagan ceremony. It is reported that the threesome have brought into their home other partners, but on the condition of mutual consent. They view their "marriage" as "sacrosanct". On the question of loving more than one wife, the head of the house believes:

> Just like a parent can love more than one child, so too can you love more than one partner. Your heart doesn't split in half, it doubles; there is an endless supply of love.[184]

## 4.2.9   Legal Developments

There appear to be emerging legal precedents which recognise unions of more than two people.

---

[181] Ibid.
[182]   http://www.independent.co.uk/life-style/love-sex/romance-passion/modern-lovers-the-sexual-body-warriors-and-pioneers-transforming-21stcentury-relationships-6700186.html  (12 February 2012)
[183] Ibid.
[184] Ibid.

In 2005, a civil union in the Netherlands was registered between one man and two women.[185] The man in the union explained that there was no jealously between the two women because they are both bisexual. He said: "I think that with two heterosexual women it would be more difficult." As noted earlier, the Netherlands was the first country to introduce same-sex marriage.

According to a member of the largest Dutch political party, a cohabitation contract between more than two people is not illegal. He said: "'Marriage' denotes 'civil' marriage, i.e. marriage as the law exclusively defines it." He further explained:

> Unlike two people who are married, "contracts that settle the cohabitation of more than two persons can have a useful ordering function.[186]

In 2012, in Sao Paulo, a public notary recognised a civil union between one man and two women. She said:

> We are only recognising what has always existed, we are not inventing anything.[187]

At time of writing, it is unknown whether this civil union – should it be tested in law – will be maintained and more widely recognised within Brazil.[188] However, this case demonstrates an emerging shift in official attitudes, moving away from the binary monogamous relationship model embodied in traditional marriage. Since a Supreme Court decision in 2011,[189] Brazil provides same-sex civil unions. This development in gay rights, signalling as it does, a departure from heterosexual marriage being the only exclusive legally recognised union, has made it possible to begin to recognise and accommodate the perceived rights of other unions like this threesome relationship.

Writing in 2003, Stan Kurtz, American writer, commentator and former fellow of the Hoover Institution, imagined what might develop if gay marriage were introduced:

> Among the likeliest effects of gay marriage is to take us down a slippery slope to legalized polygamy and "polyamory" (group marriage). Marriage will be transformed into a variety of relationship

---

[185] http://www.brusselsjournal.com/node/301 (26 September 2005)
[186] http://www.brusselsjournal.com/node/421 (1 November 2005)
[187] http://www.bbc.co.uk/news/world-latin-america-19402508 (28 August 2012)
[188] Ibid. The BBC reports that although the public notary recognised the three-way union, "it is not clear whether courts, service providers and private companies such as health insurance providers will accept the ruling."
[189] See: http://www.bbc.co.uk/news/world-13304442 (6 May 2011)

contracts, linking two, three, or more individuals (however weakly and temporarily) in every conceivable combination of male and female. A scare scenario? Hardly. The bottom of this slope is visible from where we stand. Advocacy of legalized polygamy is growing. A network of grass-roots organizations seeking legal recognition for group marriage already exists. The cause of legalized group marriage is championed by a powerful faction of family law specialists. Influential legal bodies in both the United States and Canada have presented radical programs of marital reform. Some of these quasi-governmental proposals go so far as to suggest the abolition of marriage.[190]

Kurtz cites the case of Joy Singer, who in 1996 published an article which called for the creation of a polyamorist rights movement that is to be modelled on the gay rights movement. One preliminary campaign would be to claim hospital visiting rights for polyamorist spouses.

In 1996, David Chambers, law professor at the University of Michigan, writing in the Michigan Law Review, explained how support for gay marriage would help prepare the ground for further legal changes:

> By ceasing to conceive of marriage as a partnership composed of one person of each sex, the state may become more receptive to units of three or more.[191]

In this subsection, we have sought to show the parallels between the gay rights movement and the growing movement for poly rights. In spite of gay marriage advocates accusing their opponents of scaremongering, there are clearly increasing examples designed to lift the social taboo from, and establish the "case" for, social and, ultimately, legal recognition of poly relationships.

---

[190] "Beyond Gay Marriage: The road to polyamory", 3 August 2003, Vol., 8, No. 45. http://www.weeklystandard.com/Content/Public/Articles/000/000/002/938xpsxy.asp
[191] Quoted in by Stan Kurtz, "Beyond Gay Marriage: The road to polyamory", 3 August 2003, Vol., 8, No. 45

# 5

## QUESTIONS OF FREEDOM

### 5.1    A Growing List of Precedents

A culture of intolerance towards those holding beliefs that are no longer part of an "approved list" is now increasingly common. What were once conventional values regarding traditional family life, sexual ethics and marriage are now treated with a similar uncompromising intolerance that was once meted out to homosexuals and their beliefs.

Dissent is now increasingly treated with the same repugnance and intolerance as the US Senate McCarthy Committee once treated those suspected of endorsing, or sympathetic to, communism. Increasingly, the State effectively defines 'authorised belief' in the area of sexuality and now wants to newly define the meaning of marriage so that the understanding that has stood for millennia will no longer be recognised orthodoxy.

We consider several cases in which the traditional freedoms of speech and belief have been seriously challenged, without laws actually being broken. In some of the stories that follow, the issue was connected to specific beliefs about sexual ethics, while in other cases, the facts revolved around expressing traditional views about the meaning of marriage. These are only a small fraction of the numerous cases that are becoming more common.

i.    In 2002, Mr Beales, a school head teacher, faced calls for his suspension, after telling pupils in an assembly that Christians were being "placed on trial" because of the shifts in moral behaviours that were being witnessed in society at large. He pointed out that there is a legal requirement that schools hold Christian assemblies. Mr Beales explained that Christians who give voice to beliefs about issues like marriage, homosexuality and abortion are discriminated against and labelled as bigots. In a radio interview, Mr Beales said: "We need to be aware of what is happening behind the curtain of democracy."[192]

---

[192] http://news.bbc.co.uk/1/hi/wales/2026628.stm (5 June 2002)

ii.  In 2006, a group of firemen from Glasgow were expected to take part in a gay pride event.[193] When they refused they were punished by their employers. Some claimed it would embarrass them to attend the event in uniform, while others objected for moral reasons. One fireman was demoted, which diminished his salary by £5,000. Other firemen were ordered to attend "diversity training" and received written warnings. After the internal appeals process was exhausted, the firemen's employer agreed on a settlement.

iii. In 2007, Brighton and Hove City Council made a bizarre demand on an elderly care home for Christians. The residents had to be asked every three months about their sexual orientation and to publicise LGBT events to the home's residents.[194] This agenda was apparently driven by a policy of "fair access and diversity". Care home staff were also compelled to attend a *Stonewall* presentation on LGBT issues. Pilgrim Homes, a 200 year old residential home, founded by William Wilberforce and others, notified the Council of their refusal to follow the demands, as it would contravene the religious ethos of the home.

The Council then removed £13,000 of funding, while the Care home was accused of "institutional homophobia". Just as the matter was about to go to court, Brighton Council restored the grant, while also withdrawing its accusation of "institutional homophobia".

iv.  In 2009, Mrs Howe, a Christian pensioner, complained to her local council, after she distributed Christian leaflets at a gay parade and received verbal abuse.[195] The police questioned her on the alleged grounds that she was guilty of homophobic hatred and liable to prosecution. In her letter of complaint, Mrs Howe pointed out: A representative of the legal centre that supported her case said: "People must be free to express their beliefs – yes, even unpopular beliefs – to government bodies, without fear of a knock at the door from police." It is interesting to note that Stonewall judged the response of the police as "disproportionate".

v.   In 2002, a civil registrar, Lillian Ladele refused to officiate at civil partnership ceremonies, even though she managed to coordinate her work rota with work colleagues, effectively providing her, in theory, with an opt-out. However, she lost her case in the Employment Appeal Tribunal, and the Court of Appeal upheld the decision against her. In

---

[193] 22 January 2009, Daily Telegraph.
[194] Daily Telegraph, 29 December 2008 and 7 February 2009.
[195] Daily Telegraph, 24 October 2009.

2010, her appeal was rejected by the Supreme Court.[196] A decision from the European Court of Human Rights (ECHR) is pending.

vi.  A relationships counsellor, Gary McFarlane, was sacked by Relate Avon for gross misconduct after stating that he might have a conscientious objection to providing sex therapy to same-sex couples.[197] He was motivated in this position by his Christian beliefs. While he was willing to talk to his managers about the matter should the situation arise, and although the same-sex couple scenario was merely hypothetical, McFarlane lost his appeal for unfair dismissal. A decision on his case is also pending before the ECHR.

Contrary to some media reports of this case, McFarlane never held any objections to providing general therapy to homosexuals. The issue, rather, was the provision of sex therapy. The case was tied to issues of equality, the rights of gays, and the rights of manifesting one's religious belief. Yet, between these competing rights, instead of accommodation, McFarlane's rights to freedom of religion were rejected. On a practical, non-legal level, it seems odd and incompatible to expect a heterosexual man to give sex therapy to a homosexual couple. It is no more practical than for a homosexual man to understand and appreciate heterosexual sexual techniques that are connected to therapy.

The current UK government's legal opinion on both these cases was submitted to the ECHR in September 2012, in a case, whose decision is pending. The Foreign and Commonwealth legal opinion states:

> Ms Ladele and Mr McFarlane were entitled to practice their religion in any way they chose outside their employment and were free to resign if they found the requirements of their work incompatible with their religious beliefs. Their employers were entitled to insist they provided services equally to all.[198]

It is interesting to note that in this legal opinion, the employers were "entitled" to insist that services were provided "equally to all". The underlying notion of "equality" that is at play here clearly recognises the rights of one party *at cost* of the rights of another party. This discrimination, though deemed to actually protect equality, is presumptive of *who can be favoured* in terms of their beliefs. Such a

---

[196] http://news.bbc.co.uk/1/hi/england/london/8557966.stm  (9 March 2010)
[197] For a history of the case see: http://www.christianconcern.com/cases/gary-mcfarlane
[198] Observations of the Government of the United Kingdom, the Foreign and Commonwealth, 14 October 2011.

presumption is surely a breach of the doctrine of equality that is supposedly inclusive of all beliefs.

In the McFarlane case, the 'official' belief at issue, is that there is nothing questionable – nor should there be – about providing homosexual sex therapy. Alternatively, both parties could have been accommodated so that the rights of both could be recognised in law. Instead, the law – as McFarlane's original Court of Appeal case bore out – chose to favour gay rights *over* that of religious rights. It reflects a wider socio-cultural drive that elevates the gay worldview over that of traditional Judeo-Christian values.

vii.   A Christian couple who ran a guesthouse, Mr and Mrs Bull, were fined £3,600 after they refused to offer a double room to a homosexual couple. Their "married couples only" policy was, we believe, fair and clearly not singling out homosexual couples, because it meant that cohabiting heterosexual couples would also not have been permitted to stay. In reality, couples were never asked for any proof of their status but were taken on trust. Since the court judgment, the Bulls have been directly subjected to acts of intimidation which have not been followed through by police.[199]

viii.  An Anglican lay preacher urged his parishioners to sign the Coalition for Marriage (C4M) petition, its supporters asking to retain the current definition of marriage as between one man and one woman. He was asked to stand down for two months to "let the dust settle" after a reported outcry at the Sunday service.[200] This happened despite the fact that the Church of England's official teaching affirms traditional marriage.

The lay preacher said: "I have never heard of anyone being suspended because people don't like what you said or the way that you said it." He added: "This has been one of the great strengths of the Church, that it will accept and tolerate people with different opinions. It is disappointing that some people are so narrow minded."

---

[199] See: http://www.dailymail.co.uk/news/article-1338232/We-set-claim-Christian-B-amp-B-owners-sued-refusing-let-gay-couple-share-double-bed.html (14 December 2010)
http://www.dailymail.co.uk/debate/article-1348790/Gay-couple-sued-Christian-hotel-owners-staying-true-faith-right.html (20 January 2011)
http://www.dailymail.co.uk/news/article-1348207/Christian-hotel-owners-Peter-Hazelmary-Bull-penalised-turning-away-gays.html (20 January 2011)
[200] Daily Telegraph, 4 May 2012.

ix.      Roman Catholic schools were warned by the Welsh administration that they might be breaking the law by encouraging pupils to sign the C4M petition.[201] However, education secretary Michael Gove judged that the Catholic Education Service had not broken the law, although he believed their letter to schools "unintentionally blurred the distinction between discussing issues that are a matter of faith and promoting partisan political views".[202]

The minister's view is disturbing for at least two main reasons. First, all three main party leaders have expressed their public support for gay marriage. This fact alone demonstrates that government plans to legalise same-sex marriage is not *expressed* as a *specific partisan* matter. Secondly, the question of marriage is not and never has been an essentially political or partisan issue. It is true that governments have at times brought in various laws in relation to marriage (connected to ceremonies, taxes, rules regulating divorce and so forth), but the essential nature of the institution is external to party and ideology.

x.      Advertisements appeared in national newspapers asking the public to sign the C4M petition. The Women's Institute (WI) rejected an offer to advertise the petition in their magazine.[203] The WI advertising magazine manager is reported to have told C4M: "…any promotion of your campaign could be seen as an endorsement…to members." WI felt that the campaign could "offend many of our members".

xi.      In May 2012, the Law Society agreed to stage a conference on the sensitive issue of euthanasia which, although illegal in practice, was given a public platform for the purposes of debating legal reform.[204] By contrast, the Law Society banned a colloquium with high profile speakers designed to generate debate about retaining the current definition of traditional marriage.[205]

After contracts were signed for the conference venue, the event was terminated by the Law Society on the bizarre grounds that the subject of the conference failed to conform to their diversity policy. In the former case euthanasia, which remains illegal, qualified as a topic

---

[201] Daily Telegraph, 9 May 2012.

[202] Catholic Herald, 29 June 2012.

[203] Daily Mail, 12 March 2012.

[204] Daily Telegraph, 14 May 2012, Comment by Cristina Odone.

[205] http://www.christianconcern.com/our-concerns/social/marriage-colloquium-goes-ahead-despite-attempts-to-ban-it (25 May 2012)

worthy of debate; yet debate about retaining the current law on marriage was deemed to be unacceptable for the marketplace of ideas.

Next, the Marriage conference was set to be held at the Queen Elizabeth II Conference Centre. Contracts were signed but, one day before the event, the Centre breached the contract obligations by not permitting the event. Again, the conference was also suddenly judged as being non-complaint with their diversity policy.

xii.    In July 2012, Christina Summers, a Green Party councillor, was ordered to face a party disciplinary panel, after she was the only member of Brighton and Hove City Council to vote against a council motion in support of the Coalition's plan's to legalise same-sex marriage.[206] The disciplinary panel decided to expel Miss Summers from the Green Group of Councillors, while still permitting her to sit as an Independent councillor and remain as a Green Party member.

Miss Summers, a devout Christian who is reported to be supportive of civil partnerships and gay rights, argued that it was not a requirement of equality to change the definition of marriage. The legal centre representing her said: "For a party that prides itself on equality, it is ironic that it seeks to remove Christina Summers for her views on marriage."

What is most disturbing in this case is that a vote was taken on an issue which should, in a free society, imply the right to choose to vote 'for' or 'against'. We argue that while there are party policy expectations to consider, by not allowing one of the party councillors to uphold a traditional understanding of marriage, there is a clear and flagrant breech of free speech and the so-called diversity that the Party claims to celebrate.

In view of the alarming number of cases where traditional freedoms have been questioned and censored, we ask how these freedoms will be impacted if same-sex marriage is legalised. We are also mindful of the impact the new law will have on schools and the freedoms of parents to withdraw their children from sex and relationships classes, which is still a parental right. It is already a legal requirement to mention marriage as part of relationships education, although there appears to be little evidence that many schools comply.

---

[206] Daily Telegraph, 27 July 2012. See also: http://www.christianconcern.com/our-concerns/religious-freedom/christian-expelled-from-green-group-of-councillors (20 September 2012)

The government's zeal to change the definition of marriage strongly points to a new future drive to 'educate' children about gay marriage. The belief in how equality is to be understood effectively leads us to believe that such 'education' will become commonplace in all schools. Furthermore, in view of a new tyranny of belief that is being forced upon those who dare express contrary beliefs, it seems very likely that teachers who express views about marriage being between a man and woman will be guilty of misconduct.

Aidan O' Neill QC was asked to give expert legal advice on a range of scenarios that might follow, should same-sex marriage be introduced.[207] What if parents tried to withdraw their child from school lessons which taught the history of gay marriage? The parents may want to appeal to the European Convention on Human Rights which, they would argue, allowed them to withdraw their child. But the school, let us suppose, refused the parent's request because of their legal duty to promote equality. O' Neill believes that the parents "will have little prospects of success in challenging the schools insistence that their child attend" the gay history lessons.

O' Neill points out that the Education Act 1996[208] imposes a duty on the Secretary of State "to issue guidance" which ensures that pupils "learn the nature of marriage and its importance for family life and the bringing up of children." In view of this statute, if same-sex marriage becomes law, O' Neill believes that as part of sex education, there will be a requirement to teach the "importance [of gay marriage] for family life and the bringing up of children."

## 5.2 Free Speech: A Sacred Component of Western Democracy?

Having considered some of the many disturbing cases that directly challenge or restrict freedoms of belief or speech, we are prompted to briefly consider our own wider culture, in the context of how debate is customarily treated in the public square.

Western democracies continue to be known as bastions of free speech, in sharp contrast to regimes where public dissent from official orthodoxy is either

---

[207] In a summary of his legal opinions, Mr O' Neill QC, offers a number of opinions relating to common scenarios that could typically arise throughout various sectors of society. In addition to those examples mentioned above, others include issues relating to NHS chaplains; teachers being required to read "King and King" stories; faith schools within the state sector; fostering parents; the provision of public facilities by churches who only conduct opposite-sex weddings; marriage registrars; religious gay weddings; and concerns that the established Church of England would be expected to offer same-sex marriage to couples wanting it.
http://www.c4m.org.uk/downloads/legalopinionsummary.pdf
[208] Section 403 (1A) (a)

penalised, suppressed or crushed with full force by the authorities. The 'enforcers' act either from fear, or a sincere belief in what they have come to accept is in the nation's best interests of security, stability and social welfare.

In our own ways, whether for legitimate or suspect reasons, our western societies have their own 'enforcers'. These may be driven by corporate public policy, manifested as 'in- house' rules, just as much as by rules of common and statutory law. For example, employees are subject to the company in-house rules reflecting departmental policy. Alternatively, questions involving rights, or the actions and speech of individuals, can be tested when they become the subject of court judgments.

Typically, in almost all areas of policy making and proposed legislation, issues are normally discussed in light of the evidence and arguments presented by opposing sides of the debate, which are given a roughly equal hearing. In the spirit of our democracy, public debates not merely accommodate but often actively welcome dissenting views. The "case" or body of argument made in support of a particular public issue is loosely 'governed' by certain protocols.

An issue is customarily studied by society, sometimes over many years, especially when it evokes moral concerns and generates a spectrum of controversy involving sensitive questions about human welfare, risk or harm. For example, the controversial question as to whether soft or hard drugs should be reclassified or decriminalised altogether continues to divide opinion among health experts, policy makers, commentators, elected representatives and the general public.

Although there is established law governing narcotics, it does not follow that society has reached a consensus which has brought closure to the debate. Indeed, while passions and deeply held beliefs reside on both sides, there are the users of drugs whose views, at times, contradict some of the prevailing wisdom about safety and health risks attached to drug use.

On the one hand, a gulf can be created between certain experts, and policy makers who warn against the dangers of heroin and even softer drugs such as cannabis. But on the other hand, there are the actual "voices" of users, many of whom feel entitled to indulge in pleasures they believe society ought not to regulate. To do so, they argue, restricts personal autonomy and is an unwarranted intrusion into privacy. The tension created between perceived entitlements of drug users and the anti-drugs advocates does not mean opposing views are not tolerated, even when they challenge the official status quo at any one time. Instead, our media, in diverse ways and with varying emphasis, openly accommodates dissenting views that challenge the orthodoxy being advocated by experts and public opinion formers.

An issue may be addressed in law at some level, while studies regarding the validity or merits of "the case" remain in progress. In other words, a diversity of views and arguments exist in the marketplace of ideas which are openly aired without derision, intimidation, finger-pointing or fear of arrest, prosecution or civil litigation.

The growing body of precedents (not limited to the UK) which reveal a dangerous culture of intolerance of belief is in urgent need of being addressed by the government. If diversity, as noted above, includes the wide spectrum of beliefs, then it is not for the government, public bodies or any professional organisation or mainstream media outlet to censor or penalise people whose beliefs about marriage and sexuality contravenes what is the new 'orthodoxy'.

It should be noted here in the gay rights context, as in any other matter of divergent opinions, disagreement is *not* hatred. Too often, the clear distinction between disagreement and hatred is blurred or entirely ignored. On the subject of gay marriage, advocates for traditional "one man, one woman" marriage are more and more depicted as subversive, uncivilised, hate-filled and prejudiced. One typical illustration is shown in the position of London's leading newspaper, which actively champions gay relationships; it unashamedly designates opponents of same-sex marriage as "bigots".[209] In line with an emerging political correctness, it dangerously conflates questions about "gays and gay relationships"[210] – an area that attracts regular confusion in the public square.

People who self-identify as "gay" are as much a part of the human family as any and every other individual, *irrespective* of the beliefs or lifestyle choices in question. However, this fact is to be sharply distinguished from the question of what we choose to understand as normative and leading to (or promoting) healthy relationships. Crucially, the implications of same-sex relationships reach well beyond the perceived rights of the adult parties involved. There are also parenting implications for children who are either adopted, or deliberately conceived through surrogacy, so that a child is deliberately *separated* from at least one of his or her natural biological parents.

---

[209] *The London Evening Standard*, leader page, 12 September 2012. The text stated that opposition to same-sex marriage "has attracted those with quite irrational objections and whose stance is chiefly determined by the fact that they simply don't like gays and gay relationships. Bigots, in short."
[210] Ibid

# 6

## CONCLUSION

We highlighted the fact that same-sex couples are already able to legally formalise their relationship and there are no further legal benefits to be gained if same-sex marriage is introduced. The Labour government, who introduced civil partnerships, believed the "concept of homosexual marriage is a contradiction in terms", while deeming civil partnerships as holding their own meaning and purpose, yet being clearly distinguished from "marriage". Although no one labelled the Labour government as "homophobic", it is now becoming increasingly common for opponents of same-sex marriage to be labelled as such.

We showed that there are six enduring components that define the universal and centuries-old institution of marriage: 1) one man and one woman; 2) procreative potential; 3) sexual exclusivity; 4) permanence; 5) mutual commitment and, 6) public recognition. These conditions of eligibility prevail over and above the varying cultural customs and legal rules that have been in operation at any one time. Contrary to the emerging belief that 'love and commitment" are sufficient to satisfy the basis for a "marriage", we demonstrated how this limited and insufficient test renders the proposition of "same-sex marriage" unintelligible, and therefore a category mistake.

As to the concept and practice of monogamy, we provided a body of evidence showing that gay relationships do not typically satisfy this condition, as it is understood by heterosexual married couples.

We surveyed the consensus of the many studies, showing how children raised by biological, intact, married parents achieve better outcomes overall, compared to those born to unmarried couples or single mothers.

We considered the contentious claim that gay and lesbian parenting is of equal value to opposite-sex parenting. Specifically, with regard to studies into gay and lesbian parenting, we highlighted the use of unscientific sampling methods, which makes all such research deeply flawed and therefore unreliable when used as support to validate same-sex parenting. To put it another way, the widely attested benefits enjoyed by children raised by married opposite-sex couples cannot be automatically transferred to support similar anticipated outcomes for children who are raised by same-sex parents. It is not comparing like with like in terms of data. All of which immediately raises questions for legislators and others in public life, when they are urged to uncritically accept those studies purporting to validate gay and lesbian parenting.

If marriage is a union of two persons, without reference to gender, this redefinition has disturbingly wide implications that impact society at large. It validates the erroneous notion that children do not need both a mother *and* father, thus effectively treating parenting roles as interchangeable. Such a notion, obliterating gender recognition, immediately renders irrelevant any idea of marital complementarity. But such a belief contradicts, at the very least, the clear differences in biology and reproductive roles characterising male and female.

According to the UN Convention on the Rights of the Child, as far as it is possible, children have the "right to know and be cared for" by their parents, which on a plain reading, can only be taken to refer to a child's biological parents. This right, enshrined in international law, is being ignored by governments who permit same-sex couples to create children through IVF. Such children will likely be denied knowledge of, and contact with, at least one biological parent. This is an injustice to children, which elevates the needs of adults over childhood rights.

We had regard to what is more commonly understood as "equality", and demonstrated how there are unintended consequences flowing from this flawed doctrine. A circumscribed acceptance of incestuous relationships is, for instance, a likely, though inadvertent, result that will be generated by the notion of "equality", as currently being peddled by the government and gay rights' activists.

We argued that the current understanding of equality is premised on, among other things, a questionable proposition that assumes 'sexual orientation' as being on a par with genetic traits such as skin colour, and therefore both innate and immutable. Such a belief is wholly unsupported by science and is therefore flawed. Alongside this, however, as both explained and supported by medical science, is clear evidence that homosexual sex carries serious health risks.

We examined the argument that allowing same-sex couples to marry is but another evolutionary step in marriage reform, effectively building upon past legal changes connected to the laws regulating marriage. However, we demonstrated clearly that these past changes were merely administrative in nature, and thus having no impact on the essential meaning of marriage, as an institution.

Contrary to government promises to safeguard religious establishments from being legally required to perform same-sex marriage, influential legal opinions were considered which hold that exemptions will not be able to withstand the demands of equality law.

We examined a number of defining factors embodying the rationale, used in support of gay relationships, and especially gay marriage. Poly advocates and practitioners are now appealing to these same arguments. Therefore, the "case" for recognising poly relationships is becoming more compelling – in the sense that the arguments being deployed are largely the same as those used to justify gay relationships, and especially in support for gay marriage. These parallels are not being openly acknowledged by those in the public square, although some prominent voices remain mindful of these dangers.

We finally considered a number of disturbing precedents in which traditional freedoms connected to beliefs about sexual ethics and marriage are being challenged, sometimes involving the loss of employment, censorship or even police investigation. Should same-sex marriage be introduced, legal opinion suggests deleterious impact on education will be inescapable, with teachers and parents being legally compelled to comply with the new orthodoxy.

In view of all the arguments and evidence presented in this study, therefore, we urge all those in positions of authority, and especially the government, to have more careful regard to the wider, long-term and pervasive consequences flowing from the introduction of same-sex marriage.

# BIBLIOGRAPHY

Anderson, Digby. (Ed.). (1992). *The Loss of Virtue: Moral Confusion and Social Disorder in Britain and America.* The Social Affairs Unit: A National Review Book (USA).

Balsam, Kimberly F et al. (2008). *Three-Year Follow-Up of Same-Sex Couples Who Had Civil Unions in Vermont, Same-Sex Couples Not in Civil Unions, and Heterosexual Married Couples.* Developmental Psychology. Vol. 44, No. 1, 102-116.

Barker, Meg. (2004). *This is my partner, and this is my...partner's partner: Constructing a polyamorous identity in a monogamous world.* Journal of Constructivist Psychology, 18 (1), 75-88.

Blasband, David and Peplau, Letita Anne. *Sexual Exclusivity versus openness in gay male* couples. Archives of Sexual Behavior. Vol.14, No. 5, October 1985.

Chauncey, George. (2004). *Why Marriage? The History Shaping Today's Debate Over Gay Equality.* New York: Basic Books.

Christopher, Mark. (2009). *Same-Sex Marriage: Is it Really the Same?* Leominster: Day One Publications.

Cretney, Stephen. (2006). *Same-Sex Relationships: From 'Odious Crime' to Gay Marriage.* Oxford University Press.

De Young, James B. (2000). *Homosexuality: Contemporary Claims Examined in light of the Bible and Other Ancient Literature and Law.* Grand Rapids, Michigan: Kregel Publications.

Diggs MD, John, R. (2002). *The Health Risks of Gay Sex.* The Corporate Resource Council.

Doherty, William J et al. (2002). *Why Marriage Matters: Twenty-One Conclusions from the Social Sciences.* A Report from Family Scholars. New York: Institute for American Values.

Dover, Kenneth J. (1989). *Greek Homosexuality.* Cambridge, Massachusetts: Harvard University Press.

Eskridge Jr, William N and Spedale, Darren R. (2006). *Gay Marriage: For Better or for Worse? What We've Learned from the Evidence.* Oxford University Press.

Gallagher, Maggie. (2002). *What is Marriage For? The Public Purposes of Marriage Law*. Louisiana Law Review.

Gallagher, Maggie. Testimony before the US Senate Subcommittee on the Constitution, Civil Rights, and Property Rights Hearing: "What is Needed to Defend the Bipartisan Defense of Marriage Act of 1996?" Testimony paper: "Why Marriage Matters: The Case for Normal Marriage", 4 September 2003.

Gallagher, Maggie and Baker, Joshua, K. (2004) *Do Mothers and Fathers Matter? The Social Science Evidence on Marriage and Child Well-Being*. Virginia, USA: The Institute for Marriage and Public Policy.

Giddens, Anthony. (1992). *The Transformation of Intimacy*. Stanford: Stanford University Press.

Guasp, April. (2010). *Different Families: The experiences of children with lesbian and gay parents*. London: Stonewall.

Koppelman, Andrew. (2006). *Same Sex, Different States: When Same-Sex Marriages Cross State Lines*. New Haven: Yale University Press.

Marks, Loren. (2012). *Same-sex parenting and children's outcomes: A closer examination of the American psychological association's brief on lesbian and gay parenting. Social Science Research*, 41, 735–751.

McWhirter, D and Mattison, A. (1984). *The Male Couple: How Relationships Develop*. Englewood Cliffs, New Jersey: Prentice Hall.

Moore, Kristin Anderson et al. (2002). *Child Trends Research Brief: Marriage from a Child's Perspective: How Does Family Structure Affect Children, and What Can We Do About It?* Washington DC: Child Trends.

Morgan, Patricia. (2000). *Marriage-Lite: The Rise of Cohabitation and its Consequences*. London: The Institute for the Study of Civil Society.

Morgan, Patricia. (2007). *The War Between the State and the Family: How the Government Divides and Impoverishes*. London: The Institute of Economic Affairs.

Patterson, C.J. (2005). *Lesbian and gay parents and their children: summary of research findings*. Lesbian and Gay Parenting, American Psychological Association.

Satinover, Jeffrey. (2004). *Homosexuality and the Politics of Truth*. Grand Rapids: Michigan. Baker Books.

Scruton, Roger. (2006). *Sexual Desire: A Philosophical Investigation*. London: Continuum.

Skelton, David and Flint, Robert. (2012). *What in a Name? Is there a Case for Equal Marriage?* London: Policy Exchange.

Soloman, Sondra et al. (May 2005). *Money, Housework, Sex, and Conflict: Same-Sex Couples in Civil Unions, Those Not in Civil Unions, and Heterosexual Married Siblings*. Sex Roles, Vol., 52, Nos. 9/10.

Spears, Blake and Lowen, Lanz. (2010). *Beyond Monogamy: Lessons from Long-term Male Couples in Non-Monogamous Relationships*. www.thecouplesstudy.com

Stone, Lawrence. (1979). *The Family, Sex and Marriage in England: 1500-1800*. Penguin Books.

Sullivan, Andrew. (1995). *Virtually Normal: An Argument About Homosexuality*. London: Picador.

Wardle, Lynn, D, et al (Ed). (2003). *Marriage and Same-Sex Unions: A Debate*. Wesport, Connecticut: Praeger.

**Other Documents**

*A Response to the Government Equalities Office Consultation – "Equal Civil Marriage" – from the Church of England*. (2012).

*Breakthrough Britain: Every Family Matters: An in-depth review of family law in Britain,* (July 2009). London: The Centre for Social Justice.

*Equal Civil Marriage: A Consultation*, March 2012, Government Equalities Office.

*HIV Among Gay and Bisexual Men,* (May 2012), US Centers for Disease Control and Prevention.

(1) Lilian Ladele (2) Gary McFarlane v United Kingdom. *Observations of the Government of the United Kingdom*, the Foreign and Commonwealth, 14 October 2011.

**All internet links cited in this study were accessed on October 21 2012.**